*by Robert Kelly*

Armed Descent
"The Exchanges"
Her Body Against Time
Round Dances
Enstasy
Lunes
Lectiones
Words in Service
Weeks
The Scorpions
Song XXIV
Devotions
Twenty Poems
Axon Dendron Tree
Crooked Bridge Love Society
A Joining
Alpha
Finding the Measure
Sonnets
Statement
Songs I-XXX
The Common Shore
A California Journal
Kali Yuga
Cities
In Time
Flesh Dream Book
Ralegh
The Pastorals
Reading Her Notes
The Tears of Edmund Burke
The Mill of Particulars
A Line of Sight

*Editor*

A Controversy of Poets

# Robert Kelly

# THE
# LOOM

*Los Angeles*
**Black Sparrow Press**
*1975*

This poem, all and some, is dedicated to Helen. Her living presence made a space, cosmos, inside which the mental events and narrative acts of this poem were free to occur. Without her I could not have written this poem. Without her care, I doubt whether a text, let alone so accurate a text, could have become public. It is not just accuracy of eye that's involved, but her precision of ear and understanding that guided me *katà kairón* through a three-year ocean of revision.

THE LOOM was composed in 1971 and 1972 in Los Angeles, while I was Poet in Residence at the California Institute of Technology. I want to thank Professor David Smith and Dean Robert Huttenback for luring me to Cal Tech, and for their very generous understanding whereby my teaching schedule was made so reticulated that I could slip easily through and find myself out in the open, with light and time to approach and work through so long a poem, free in the time of my mind. My thanks also to President (now Emeritus) Reamer Kline of Bard College for a grant that allowed the copying of a working version of the text. Major periods of revision were the Fall of 1972, January 1973, and the Winter and Spring of 1974-75.

I owe special gratitude to Clayton Eshleman, whose comradely vigilance and care embraced the years of composition and revision, and from whose reading of the poem my own sense of its inner nature has grown.

To the editors of the following magazines I owe thanks for presenting trial drafts, passages, versions, from one or another stage of the poem's coming into being: *Caterpillar* (Clayton Eshleman and Caryl Reiter), *Io* (Richard Grossinger and Lindy Hough), *The California Quarterly* (Elliott Gilbert), *The Bard Review* (Benjamin La Farge), *Ikon* (Jonathan Post, Harold McGee and Robert Harmon), *Active Anthology* (1975) (George and Susan Quasha), *Boundary 2* (William V. Spanos).

LIBRARY OF CONGRESS CATALOGING IN PUBLICATION DATA

Kelly, Robert, 1935-
    The loom.

    I. Title.
PS3521.E4322L6       811'.5'4      75-25862
ISBN 0-87685-234-7
ISBN 0-87685-233-9 pbk.

*for my lady Helen*

# CONTENTS

*There are thirty-six untitled, numbered sections. In this Table of Contents, each section is accompanied by a bracketed phrase more in the nature of one-line commentary than title.*

1.   [To find a place]                                        11
2.   [A place to talk : The Table]                            23
3.   [Lady Isabella & the Mind's Geography]                   37
4.   [Ariadne Wakes]                                          59
5.   [Korinna & the Inside of the Sea]                        67
6.   [Delbrück's Version : The Party]                         82
7.   [Language]                                               90
8.   [Coming to the Nurse]                                    96
9.   [Essay on Form]                                         109
10.  [The Old Man of the Mountain]                           116
11.  [A Labor of Herakles, as it turns out]                  124
12.  [Theory of Narrative]                                   143
13.  [The Djinn's Experiment]                                155
14.  [Pain : Dream of the Burnt Heart]                       168
15.  [for Helen]                                             184
16.  [I change my mind]                                      185
17.  [Her Woof]                                              213
18.  [His Wood — Jesus's Song to his Rood]                   222
19.  [To say it all]                                         232
20.  [Sabbath in the Nucleus]                                237
21.  [The Garden of the Lame God]                            245
22.  [The Hallway of Isis]                                   254
23.  [Across to the other side : a tenderness]               272

24. [Encounter with the Anima]                          284
25. [Still Life : the Resentment of Women]              295
26. [Obsession of the House]                            306
27. [The crow in his own moment at last flies away] 317
28. [Episode on Mars]                                   325
29. [The Garden Itself]                                 346
30. [The Tinctures of Polyphemus]                       371
31. [To find the natural]                               380
32. [Goldberg Variations : The Cat]                     381
33. [Vesica Piscis & Holy Wood]                         384
34. [The Vixen]                                         393
35. [The Voice]                                         396
36. [Building of the Temple]                            401

# THE LOOM

# 1

To find a place
to talk to you
or find
a talk
to place you in,
natural contexts
growth & form
fold, calm hands
of a man
hearing music,
hears it
as it is,
fold & unfold,
two rhythms two
motions,
                place
& talk.
We could call them
City & Language,
be Dante, be
tuscan or be simpler,
a place & talk,
no time, Time doesnt
come here, it *is*
our here & all
our everywhere,
force, last energy
the scientists
will construe —

starting with
I love you
where it all began
& that formulation
still waits their
reverentest minds
(will it come that way,
will they ever require
that much
sense of themselves?
before an answer comes
they lose their breath,
o technology
you are so asthmatic).

Call it an overture
to ask,
or a *yod* slipped
after a consonant
to soften it, ease
a front vowel in,
sweet tongue
fishing
shallows of the mouth.
Opening
to ask a place
& talk in place
& all outside
that way let in.

There is so much
to remember
but less need to —
the fire
does not memorize,
what it burns

is our best archive,
fire
a wonder
of coming back
today to today
o holy now
within the holy
always, always,
*und ewig* (Mahler's
paradox, to die away
on that word,
to let the last echo
of Sometime
resounding in Notime
be Always, *ewig*,
*ewig*, soft Austrian
palatal g,
a hush
on Nature falls).
A week passes,
the logarithms
of persuasive
oblivion lift
each day away
& store it, each day
taking less space
than each one before.
My Now reduces,
the past enlarges
until I lose
even the dumb
pains of this minute
in the receding tide.
A few things are left,
agates in pools,
starfish trapped, a crab

no bigger than a quarter
very bright red.
What sea is this?
We saw them dried
for sale in Oregon.
No sales tax —
that pleased you,
still some chance
of private transaction
possible
between two people,
no State looking on —
it's not the cash of it
but the surveillance
bringing everything
to such a tedious
formal, tax, it's all
one more tool
of Remember.

So the tide moves
& what it drags
out draws
in again, awash
in the never
ending interval
between high & low tides
where the past that we
remember
moves landward
into the solidity
of beckoning Order
away from the freedom
we have inly so
intently experienced,
those seashore

moments when we know
we *are* at a shore & it *is*
a betweenland.
Now find the nurse
below the sea
where all the dead men
rest uneasy,
mumble nonsense
through my teeth
as I try to sleep
apart from that dreary
no-color queendom
where lost things go,
our cradle, our hokey
Rosebud sleds,
plumes of nostalgia
wormy now,
the Utterly Oral,
homeland of suck.
We understood that:
that music best
we make between ourselves
or hear there,
hear,
& everything else
distracts, blurs
the intense outline
of what we have
worked, still
how much longer work
to flesh out,
a marriage,
as if it could
be anything other than
ourselves together.
Then where's this

Magnificat I hear now
over the portable
from last summer
in the Berkshires,
as if even the lousy
machines remembered
& I have no past
except the thought of you
a quarter-hour back
when I walked through the room
& saw you, both of us
a little shy
because of how you were
midway in arranging
your incredible hair.
And you had your ears
plugged against the music!
What could be clearer
than that? And still
I go on listening,
overorchestrated, chorus
too big,
twisting solemnity
with a capital Bach
all over the clear
arteries of the music,
the tourniquet our in-
tentions can be,
strangling what we love
too imprecisely.
I'm not talking about
performance,
but the scales of size
a man has to know
clearly
not to botch everything;

education
should be schooling
in proportion.
Nothing else
can be known.

So the *amen*
makes it calmer,
the applause
comes on,
they're being thorough
before they go
out into the night
where the music
has its last
chance in them.
The night
itself is kind.
Thank God
for that or
whoever it is puts
berries in bogs,
cherries on cherrytrees.
Is that music?
And all the rest
is music too,
even their thoughts,
serenade of their
fantasies going downhill,
damp on their clothes
from the grass,
grass found next
morning dried out stuck
in the shoe, the world
of adventure trying
to get in

between sole & last,
reality hotfoot,
that's music.
*Parsifal* begins, Act II,
the radio still
but you're up &
listening now,
your world, the garden
of temptation,
redemption. As ever
the music
clearer than text.
Kundry, your sister,
who bared her right breast
suddenly at suffering
Jesus dragging his cross,
half to mock & half
(more dangerous)
with tears in her eyes
to offer him a suck,
that he might drink
again
the milk of generation
& all it means,
call off his work
in the kindness of her kind.
Even his curse on her
redeems her: Linger
till I come again,
woman eternal jewess,
linger
until I come
at the end of the world
to be healed in you,
in no one but you,
& I will be your mother

as you joked to be mine,
miriam tit tit
soft woman linger
until the end
*when the male*
*becomes female & the female*
*male, & we move*
*naked at last*
*beyond the garments*
*male & female one*
*& none.*
   That's the promise
in Thomas's gospel,
dug up
at Nag Hammadi
by angelic instruction,
brought to light in our
time, for my need.
And Klingsor's garden
of mechanic forms
passes away in light,
light of words
glances upward
from an ancient page
free of tradition,
a naked word
to begin us anew.

This is for the
sexes. Kundry, soft
insolent woman.
Parsifal unable to touch
her flesh
because of compassion
searing the sky,
blood of Amfortas

spurts from his desire,
man & woman will be
one, & none,
when compassion
does not mean sharing
but a loving silence
hears everything,
no mind
dumb to that dialogue
& no heart deaf.

What survives to us
is our matter,
pearl from dunghill,
the beginning.
*Erlösung*, to be
loosed from every
locked condition,
locked part of me
that does not mean.
That does not love.

"Amfortas! those
wounds" of his —
that's what the hero
sees flaring
from her seductions,
blood of her blood
her unclosable
wound, womb/wound,
ax-bite
& all the rest
of that mythology.
But the ax
is double, bites
in man & woman,

the wound
gives pleasure,
felix culpa & rose
higher on every
thorn, throne,
thorn-throned
rose of the world.

Mythology:
I think it's given
as headstart,
heritage of syntax
I can use
until I grow
to make my own.
Those wounds are in us,
& the blood
is so musical
we fall for it
over & over, never
remembering
what runs in blood
quicksilver of
as blood
runs in us —
its *life*,
its life
it would be our
heaven to share.
Share this.

It's simpler
than I can
remind myself to know.

We need a soap

to float off
the clung
associations, film
of past impressions.
By now I should
put them all
on tarot cards,
all the by now smooth
polished image pebbles
left in my mind,
snapshots
who would be you.

Helen, whose name
Homer puns on, to mean
the woman who destroys,
sets fire, ruins
the fabric
of that paranoid
hero society: Helen
destroy Kundry.
Destroy Wagner.
And if I am not more
than the impress,
sore spot left
in flesh by those
gleaming pebbles,
no more than my
images, Helen,
destroy me.

# 2

A place to talk.
I've always loved tables,
a natural gamecourt
to lean & draw on —
to have something
between us
common to us both
& thus uniting.
When I'm working alone
I like to be at table
in dialogue with book,
or better with what comes
into my head to write
from the source of source,
wild fountains back of old
poetry, the Muse behind the muse.
And tables
make us sit down — a good &
human stance.

He sits at the table.

*Balanced on thighs & soles*
*backbone upright*
*head high above,*
*he looks out over Sumeru*
*& laughs at the gods*
*fucking their shaktis,*
*laughs at the white glow*

*behind them*
*where the milk*
*of all their orgasms*
*neither reveals nor opaques*
*the unconditioned brightness,*
*no-source of all source.*

I'm happier in cotton
than in silk or tigerskin
but I get the point, I sit
there night after night,
sometimes bent over the notebook
sometimes watching the faint
breeze agitate the ivy
thinking of girls.
Then I look up
from what I see
& see.

Where I miss a man
is not getting him & me
around a table —
            Charles & me
in his kitchen, making that
rickety table dance
all over the floor, wound up
eight feet from the door one
night, had him
halfway into the bedroom,
bookroom, then he worked me
back to the door. Then I edged
him to the stove & he remembered
coffee. All of this with no
will but Will
to move us
as it moved his talk

higher & more worth
struggling after than
any man I heard;
but that table was like
the saga bench the Finns
rock back & forth on,
hands clenched, drawing &
yielding — that is
how it is when men talk,
& better to have the gesture
ready. Or the table
set,
    Third Surface
between the surfaces of our minds
where the whole
mystery of talk
bounds & needs
the bounce. The shared
preoccupation. I'm no friend
of heart-to-hearts; for heart
to speak to heart you need
a table. A body. A body
of work. A trade. A box
of swiftian tools.

The Third
is magic —
it unlocks the heart.
Heart to heart is dumb squish.
We need
the artifice of order, something
to talk around,
an obstacle. A stump.
How to find a
*language* inward,
true dialectic inways.

How to find
a table inside me.
Tabula. So far the Image
(flat as a playing card,
simplified, arcane
in its smoothness)
has done the work.
Something inside
to tell my question
from its answer:
I have heard voices
& I have believed. But how can I
turn inward, elbows firmly
planted, the table
rapping, this
is all about tables, seance
in the head.
The voice instructs me:
my inwards
is outside,
my table
stretches before me blank,
my need to fill it,
the poem, always the poem.
Inside-out man.
A voice from inside me
I hear far away,
up the canyon, over the mountain,
over the ocean, Write Me,
Write Me
            (a woman's voice then,
that I attend her necessities,
that female presence
in me or of me
that also I have found outside,
anima mea),

inside outside,
I lean on the paper
& talk to it
& it talks back
the habits of my english
& all trade of words
I've learned or guessed —
oracle of lines, *not*
between the lines but the lines
themselves,
flex & fall,
sonority, the count.
The table
is not drenched with gore,
no streamers
flap overhead.
The inside
is projected, deep
*hypothesis*
*that a poem*
*could exist*,
blank page, & on it
everything I know
to call down of the hour
into words
(hearing it always
inside me, maybe not the full
of it but enough
to take a hint)
& then the completed poem
opens
to me, opens me,
instructs.

So the poem
stays out there

in the world
& forgets about me.
Maybe somebody else
can use it as a table
or to prop a table
when his own falters
or he finds
his thoughts wont stay in place
in the hour
of his desire.
One of my books
had pictures in it
& a deep-blue
shiny cover—a young
man gave a copy
to his red-haired girl,
dropped it by surprise,
a present, in her lap.
Blue / shine / redhair / lap,
& it was mine—first lust
of ownership lost
in the thrill of that
interpreted touch.
Because the lap's a table
& yet it is & yet it is.
I could never be a protestant—
they lack all sense of altars
confuse
altars with dining rooms
& put their talk
in a pulpit. The talk
should be on the table,
where we're told to put our cards,
words, emblems
of our in fact condition.
The bread & wine

are private, a mouth
goes anywhere—let's sit
& talk
& worship
at your lap
which is always where it is
& hides when you travel.
Lap communion.
Lap of reverence
where in the softest
contour
an angel of geometry
makes me god
by leading me
a necessary road.
Is you, Helen, for me,
I persist.
As if I would define you
by my desire?

There comes to mind
that image of Pharaoh
Mycerinus & his wife,
her thighs instructive as yours,
their hips not quite touching.
Each folded in self,
hands folded
as if in hearing or containment—
two lovers, side by side.
Their powers are
balanced, from a shared
center they look out
with immensely
different eyes,
the man the woman
seeing never the same

landscape. He
does not understand her,
she does not understand
him; it is perfect.
In their love & sharing
there's no room
for the complacent analyses
that pass for understanding
between the sexes.
Men & women
are different species
from different
places, join
a little
for their work on
earth.
         You are
my Venus. Other planet,
other race
someways symbiotic with my own.

Mycerinus & that woman
stand there
looking on the worlds
from their separate minds.

*Unum caro*, they used to say,
one flesh, yes, it is in flesh
that you & I are one
but no business
elsewhere
can unite
the magnificent
difference.
Body also is workshop, tool.
Neither woman aping man

nor man woman (we are so
coy sometimes)
neither aping nor disdaining,
we go separate ways
the same road?
                    Who knows
where the road leads
until the road
folds up like Christ's moon,
an old scroll
we have read to the end.
And then I guess we enter
by one gate
the energy of time
& become one with it
who can never be one now,
who always need tables.

Beds. Lampshades.
The habit is you
cook for me, keep coffee
ready all the time.
I make your morning coffee
since I hate to lie abed
& you love waking slowly:
the difference
could not be more profound
but let's not make
too much of it. I will not
pry here. I love you
even waking, & the strong hot
coffee from the macchinetta
in yellow cup
from my hand, still too early
in the day to be steady,
passes to yours, very weak,

vague, moving slowly
towards the cup, sometimes
as you begin to drink,
your fingers stroke my hand.
Nothing more than that
& no more needed.
Recognitions
in a sphere.
(See, we may have to
move on to geometry,
the round kind, not the skinny
plain of Egypt
studded with mark-lines,
boundary stones.)
We talk
in all kinds of ways.
Ah, you poem,
you ambisexual thing!
Fatti maschi, parole femine,
deeds male, talk female,
& if so, if so,
look at the poem,
that *deed of words* —
an agreement shared
between the races,
a gift
between.
This they knew
at Montségur.
In Languedoc. At
Arles. At Tolosa.
At Albí.

The first poem
I wrote from you
knew all this.

It was called *Tabula*
for reasons
then not clear.
It seemed to be about
a morning when
worried about money
I drove to town grumbling
over the crest of Whaleback
then down on Voorhis'
pastureland I saw his
morgans running red gold brown
after a spring rain.
My heart lifted, cloud off,
& I remembered a girl
who last night
had brought peonies to the house,
a girl tender & tough & knowing
her way around, innocent
because busy all day long
with the motions of her heart.
You had come
not trapped
in heart or head
by training or society.
That was the first
wonder, that you were free,
sat in my house, rode
beside me when I drove you
(another night) home,
while I panted for you
with as yet undiscriminating
appetite, you were free
to refuse everything
but the specific.
Another day I drove
with my left hand.

My right rested, *rested*
tight between your thighs.
It was the first day of my life.
Why. Not the first woman or
first thighs, but that's
how it felt. Not felt. Was.
First day of my life,
in your lap.
In society we grow to believe
there is some holiness or worth in being one.
From the first touch of you
I knew
I had the strength to be separate.

My heart is hubris
to go beyond
the simple pump
& move
the currents of
divine intellection
through the cellular
(we are taught to
think of it) cosmos.
The heart is the only hybrid
then, not the child
who varies the powers
of his immediate
sources, but the heart
four-chambered
(the elements)
& double-rhythm,
systole, diastole,
each faithfully recorded
light years away
in the smallest
capillary,

current of the heart.
So Mycerinus & the woman
look, full-faced,
like the heart:
half male half female
upper body lower body,
the four chambers
united
not in what they are
(there is no
existential union,
a marriage is always
double,
dance of two wills,
never one, it is
blasphemy to make one
will of those two stars),
the King & the Queen
united
in the fact of what they do.

Every curve of the Queen's
body knows my mind.
Out of memory
I follow her thigh
now leads me to
your lap. Poignance
of those curves
that move me more
than any shape
or color I have seen.
From heart over hip to
mound of thigh, gentle,
the draw between.
Along this line
the upper & lower

chambers of the heart
are connected.
The central Gateway
is the place between
man & woman,
                the space
called into being
by their closeness
touching, touching close
but always the distance
between. Valve,
all power from that distance.
Their shared
separate powers,
curve under the Queen's
right breast, shadow
between her & his left arm
where the heart beats
strongest,
pulse or throb;
in that betweenspace
rose the power of Egypt
Upper & Lower,
two crowns
never
be yielded to one.

# 3

This is the meat
of day & night in the street
as once men asked
does the Spirit proceed
from the Father & the Son
or through the Son —
they knew
what the difference meant.
Or could mean
to them.
Now it sounds
just like words
(of like substance?
of same substance?)
but I can imagine
in that Byzantium
those questionings
were searchings
within a circuitry
we still carry in our heads,
Boehme clearer than any
Christian ever on this —
In the name of the Father in me
& of the Son in me
& of the Holy Spirit in me.
This is our world
& it has no end.

I think on these hot days
of when a city

ate theology
(before Justinian
destroyed the equity of gold)
& their god-information
was everyday pentecost,
flame brain,
the fire of the Spirit
lighting up the black abyss
where the Father lurks
*whom we would never know*
*did not the Son*
*in his hot mercy make bright those depths.*
Where can I look for him
better than in what I carry around,
this spread of country, this me?
And that is a scope
or scale of work,
for me to look down
& report what I see.
I will give
all the places
he might be between.

Get away with it,
the holiday
arching over us,
bunting sky
with never a snowflake in it,
grisaille,
a strange smell.
Like hell gate, that point
on the San Diego Freeway
heading north
when the cool air of the coastal plain
stops
abrupt

& my arm out the window at 1 a.m.
got the blast of still intact
inland heat
before we even reached the crest
& looked down on that great valley.
It moves me oddly, cant say why,
clear night & the San Fernando
valley below us like a galaxy
limited, a band
stretching infinitely west
but some hint of border
far away to the north —
& it's all
made one
by light,
interconnecting,
city,
a masque of energy.
So no sooner
had I determined
to look inside
when a night valley
filled with intuition
drafts itself
under my glance, sketchmap
of the outside, Credo,
borrowed
from my physical stance,
Look Down.
I remember how Chuck Stein was clear
that to meditate on tarot trumps
meant the body
had to act out
every stance
pictured on the card
to understand what it saw.

To look for God
look like God.
To find water in the earth
cut your dowsing fork
from one of water's trees
(hazel, willow, cottonwood)
& hold it as if backwards
turned in your hands
so that the lawfulness
of hidden water
deep below the earth
will act upon the fork
to make it flow straight
as water does
always obedient
to its one possibility.

Our loveliest jewel
is to begin anywhere.
Bay of Naples on my mind,
volcano plume, a boat
thucks across the smooth hot
water & the breeze
is what we'd rather not,
hot, & there are indolent women
wobbling on deck,
a cruise out of sight
moving (wrong time of day)
late afternoon
right into the sun.
Eyes wrinkled closed
but sweat in the furrows
thick, like the olive oil
we think of in this place.
An egg
in the palm of my hand,

dull shell, getting sweaty,
a few cracks already,
hardboiled this morning
soon to be metallic,
will I eat or let it sink
I toss it
it sinks, bobs, rises, settles.
History of an Egg in the Bay at Naples
in three volumes, octavo,
illustrated with curious views of the natives
& seven appendices
each in smaller print than the one before.
Graphs maps tables & charts.
We're moving west, slow journey
to Palma in the Balearics,
unlikely. An old man, a Christian
but wearing a turban, bends on the rail
beside me: "My name
is Ramon Lull, & men
have ceased to believe in my existence.
I invented this machine you're looking at."
—What machine?
"The sea, the cybernetic
movements of the waves
or hadnt you noticed.
Before my time, the Mediterranean
moved like any ocean,
a larger but less intelligible machine.
Pretending to be a missioner
intent on converting the Moor
I crossed it repeatedly,
way out there where we're going,
between Mallorca & Africa,
& on each crossing laid
in careful order
certain crystals & dusts of metals,

feathers & lockets & herbs
into the sea
in such a way
its rhythm, through the whole Mare Nostrum,
began to change.
Now a man who knows what he's doing
(rare!)
& who can understand the workings
of my machine
(not hard, once he realizes
that it is a machine —
that's always the problem,
isnt it, but I wander)
& who has a problem to solve
(o rarely!), why such a man
can read off his answers as he sails.
He sets his problem out
by the way he trims his sails —
he reads their shadows, reads
his own shadow. Time of Day."
—You're just an old poet (I said),
I've read some of you,
your mantic wheels, your concentric
boxes of memory.
"That's what I let them think,
knowing that my final computer
was too big for them to find.
God taught me that."
—Did you ever convert any Moslems?
"I hardly remember
what that means. I loved God
very much in those days, like a young lover
always doing crazy things.
But we've been married so long
I love him no less
but I know now

that Love, He, She, God I mean,
does not submit
to any definition
whereas young lovers
are fond to believe
their extravagant words — poemas,
you understand —
are eligible to define
the object of their holy love.
Hence all my eagerness
to make converts & definitions,
supposing God at that time
to be as committed
as I was to the path by
which I had come to him.
Why should he be?
He's where he is
& we move
in whatever way occurs to us
or opens to us
& the way itself
has meaning
only from the goal thereof.
The Russians understand my work
better than you westerners
because materialism
is a cleaner religion
than the lenten soups
you american scientists
make of the world, not quite matter
& not quite mind.
You make me sick.
Forgive me if I'm personal."
—I'm not a scientist.
"Dont be too sure. That way
of looking at the world

stares out of your speculative eyes."
—I'm a poet, as you were.
"They're the same thing, dont even
americans know that yet?"
—I find your observations
excessively general. I detest
approximation. There is a clear
difference between poet & scientist.

But my companion moved away,
up towards the prow.
I felt at the moment too proud
to follow him. Old men make me sick.
No, he said that, young men
who have not understood
the difference, & what it's worth
& what it's *not* worth,
made him sick.
Is that what he said?
I wanted to find a lady,
a surer companion.
I found her under a canopy
starboard, shielded
by cabin & awning from the sun.
She was the Lady Isabella
travelling with her white clothes
to the Isle of Mallorca.
I eased my weight
into the creaky slatted deckchair
beside her, holding my breath
lest it crumble & thus foil
my casual address. Hello.
She gave me a sweet smile
aged thirty-nine. She is attractive,
the skin of her neck
in good condition, her hands

shapely & rather large,
her skirt is rather short
so I know I'm among friends,
a sister, hello, hello.
"I am the Lady Isabella de Cabeza.
I was born in Philadelphia
while it snowed. For that reason
in every season
I do wear white.
I have many lovers, some slim & young,
others older & thicker.
In Naples they call me La Verità."
—I will be an easy mark for your frankness
(I said) & an easier mark for your charms.
"You are courtly, fat man;
it will serve you well
in the Queendom of Mallorca
to which our vessel tends.
My mother heads an Institute there,
the Cabeza Foundation, have you heard of its work?"
—Not I. "It is our purpose
to apprehend subjectively
the operations of the mind
as it perceives the brain.
Do I make myself clear?"
—Not entirely. "I supposed not.
My thoughts too are somnolent since lunch,
fettucine I think they call them,
better in Rome but passable in Naples.
What did you eat for lunch?"
—Some eggplant salad, fresh cheese, a loaf
of twisty bread with sesames.
"Will that permit you
easy evacuation?" —I'm counting
on the oiliness of the eggplant sauce.
"I trust your confidence

is not deceived. The morning will tell.
I find it important
to take an interest in my bowels,
a healthy clean anus
is so sensitive an index
to various kinds of pleasures,
perceptions, states of mind,
dont you agree?" —Do you refer
to anal intercourse, neapolitan
specialty that it's supposed to be?
"Partially to that, but do not so
eagerly anticipate, or restrict
your thoughts to sex." —Forgive my
parameters. "It is nothing.
Let me continue about the Institute.
My mother, Lady Consuela,
some years ago (while at the court
of King Alfonso —I was a child
of her late middle age) was an early
devotee of the work of Dr Freud.
During her sessions with patients
(mostly the lower echelons of the
Bourbon-Parmas) she conceived the idea
that the mind or intellect
is conscious of being
not only in a body
but in a head —a brain. So she proposed
to solve the deepest problem
—I do not exaggerate —
confronting philosophy in our day:
the relations between the Mind & the Brain.
English expresses the distinction exactly,
other languages less well.
How fortunate you are an american!"
—I have sometimes thought so too.
"Now the brain

46

gives its reports internally
but can be persuaded —electrode—
to report objectively
directly, electrically,
to the world outside.
We all know that.
How can the Mind
report?  Language & the arts
& society have been its usual
means, & the Mind
dances in a delighted trance
of conceiving itself outside
body & brain, out here, in a world
of shared statements & shared
understandings."
                         —You sound like me now.
"No wonder.  Now my mother's intuition
was that the Mind
could be persuaded
through personality
to spy on the treasure house of the brain,
could sneak in & learn
where all the images & learned techniques
are stored, the data,
could learn
to move through the brain
freely, thus mastering it.
To free the mind
from the circuitry
of the brain: that's the motto
of the Institute."
—I am very impressed.

Lady Isabella
has gotten handsomer
all the while she's been speaking;

I hoick the chair closer.
—Tell me more.
"Two of us
are on board. It may explain
to say we own this ship, the
*Palma de Juventud* — or at least
it is on loan to us
from the Marques de So,
the Catalonian magnate. He too
is aboard. He is my lover
at the moment. Fortunately for you
(since you have an eye for that)
the extreme morbid jealousy
of the Castilian
does not extend to well-born Catalans,
distinguished by their indifference
to established *Bürgerwerten*."
—Your German accent is splendid,
especially the Rs. Have you lived there?
"Certainly not. No friend
of the mind visits Deutschland.
Bavaria perhaps. As a girl
I knew the elderly Dr Strauss
& helped him defend
himself from the friendliness
of the american liberators.
He called me Daphne, after his opera,
though I assured him
neither it nor she were my style.
With him my mother & I
made our earliest experiments.
I was sixteen, but she was aged.
Together we recorded
Dr Strauss's subjective impressions
of where the various musics
lived in his head. It seems

he was geographied
by tonality, each key signature
occupying a different
sector of his head."
—Sector?
          "Yes, part of the solid, the
'colloid' of the brain. Are you cognizant
of spherical geometry?" —Hardly.
"Well, perhaps that is best.
After all, only the subjective
is of any value.
All the rest
is preposterous theory,
& as such
conditioned by time.
Harvey bathed in the light of the moon,
did you know that, for his gout.
Podagra. It should be clear to you
that what passes as objective
is always contingent
on the preconceptions of the measurer
(or of the machine he constructs),
& thus conditioned by time, history,
*his* time. Hence, in all rigor,
not objective at all.
Now the subjective alone
has the value
of transcending time. And by a paradox
of being utterly personal
it transcends the limitations
of cultural presupposition.
Do I make myself clear?"
—I have often thought so.
"In this age, not unjustly called
the Age of Relativity,
only the subjective response

49

has any useful value.
It is with something like horror
that we read the blunders
of what passed for objective science
through the 18<sup>th</sup> & 19<sup>th</sup> centuries,
even in my mother's lifetime
physicists at Oxford
lectured on the luminiferous ether.
When we turn to physiology or medicine,
it is appalling
to see what a Claude Bernard
took for absolute
unquestionable fact—they were all misled,
are still being misled,
by the myth of the machine
which they revere & fear
forgetting all the while
they've filled their meters & measures
with preconceptions
hidden in their shared time.
Only the Conscious Subjective
makes the kind of sense
that will be as useful in 500 years
as today. Galileo is an antique toy,
Montaigne is a comrade, a contemporary,
who never fell
for the brass choir of the Absolute."
—I think you've made your point, I'm
sure of it. I am utterly convinced.
But what do you do? "Do? Who?"
—You at the Institute . . .

                          "We record
what men tell us of their heads
& how it feels
to be inside them.
Think of a pretty girl."

50

—That's easy. Chopping an axe handle
the model is not far away.
"You misapply the quotation,
but do what I say." —I'm thinking.
"Where in your brain do you see her?"
—Wait a minute, let me, yes,
she's a brunet I knew in Canada,
she's in a yellow two-piece dress.
I see her just to the right
of a line drawn from back to front of my skull,
sagittal suture is that? yes, just
right of there, towards the front a little
& not at the surface, down a little,
not deep. Here, give me your finger.
(I press her fingertip
to the part of my scalp
above where the image rises.)
"That is our first experiment. I will
record it later, in the special book
we compile for each subject, at
the Institute. You will stay with us,
of course, at Palma?"
                        —I had thought
to stay at a hotel. "They crawl with
tourists. Stay with us. What was her name?"
—I'd rather not say.
"Why not?" —The name
would give the image too much power.
"Oh you play those games with yourself too?"
—Too? Do you do that? "Of course not,
I'm a woman
who knows her mind
in some detail. All the poignance
of image & name
is old stuff with me now. I meant
by 'too'

51

that most people do,
protect themselves, I mean, that way
from the powers that course in the brain
& would spill
over into conscious mind
hurting or wounding."

During her words
some steward was banging a bell.
We rose & I gave her my arm
which she accepted
from another century. We went down
to dinner.  At table
were the Marques de So (somewhat
ratty for all his wealth, a peppery chinbeard
a white suit, elderly but not too old),
Professor Umbekanz from Johannesberg,
a dodderer & skeptic it seemed, his
adorable grandchild of fourteen, Matoesje,
who was clearly violently in love with
the arrogant Professor Fratz
whose godlike face & long blond hair
would at first make one doubt
he held the chair
of Sociometrics at Aberystwyth
on loan from Kiel.
His English was excellent, he prided himself
on his vanguard views & enlightened
youthfulness, had dropped acid
just after his orals, owned BMWs
both car & cycle. He wore tie-dyes
& never lectured from notes.
Sister Maris Stella completed the table,
an american nun who played the guitar.
On the other side of the room,
Ramon Lull was dining tête à tête

with an attractive Tunisian girl —
I saw him pressing
pamphlets into her hand, inscribing
some of them & in others
apparently making textual corrections.
Two spies exchanging news.
Poor Matoesje's googoo eyes
soon filled with tears
at a particularly brusque
rejoinder from Fratz.
She fled the room & old Umbekanz
muttered about black water fever.
My flan had a fly in it.
I stopped eating & forced
down a certain nausea,
fixing the quivering
slop with my eye.
A third maybe of the fly was
visible, some feet sticking
out of the caved-in flan-side.
As the mass jellied, it had the look
of an idea caught in the mind.
*Located* in the mind
but does it matter
where the fly exactly was
in the colloid?  That was the crux
of the whole thing.
I looked at Isabella, lured her eyes
to look down at my flan. She saw the fly
as I idly turned the saucer
to show it. Her eyebrows went up.
I wondered if she'd follow my chain of
inference. She leaned over
& under the table put her
left hand on my knee — I felt her several rings
dig in. "You're wrong. It does matter."

—Let me speak frankly, Isabella.
I have been lonely, that is why
I even think to come with you
& visit your Institute. My way
has always been to keep silent
until the mind
chose to disclose itself
in the deed of the poem.
But now I'm lonely, & I dont
believe in this Europe at all.
I wanted to go to a land
where Europe was unknown,
or if known then defeated.
I moved to California & found
the house we lived in
had a Gainsborough on the wall,
Gainsborough! Do you understand,
Lady Isabella? I am lonely. Artaud
had done with the judgment of God.
That is not enough, & in the flames
of his last days he knew it; to have done
with the judgment of men,
their opinions calendars ambitions fears —
have done with them
& hope
against all conviction
that one day the ultimate air will open
& each of us
will only be alone,
alone,
in the incredible beauty
of a multiplicity
of different separate *ones* —
to invent
the plural of one, do you
possibly understand me?

I am lonely, Isabella,
& so your foolish plans
seem to play into my hands.
To know the brain,
that secret cradle, that lair
where the dragon Mind lurks
darting in & out, guarding
*my* amassed treasures, I would even
accept this childish
premise of subjective brain geography
to get closer to the root.
Root? Glint of gold,
the ring
that Wotan
had to cast
upon the pile
because Fasolt
could still see
the merry
eye of Freya
where all the
love & good
of this world
reflect
& by their play
in her bright eye
deny
all knowledge
that is not love.
Now I must find that treasure,
find the ring
& pluck it out,
so I can see her eye.
Do you understand me
Isabella?

"I see no need for opera, Robert.
I understand what you're saying
but you can speak to me
in your own person,
not with borrowed stories."
—That's so easy to say—I am nothing
but what I have amassed,
so far my Mind
is nothing but
the impress of the brain,
its factual
accumulations, its greed.
"Dont talk any more.
I understand you
but you're saying it all wrong.
Everything you've just said
is blunder. When you say you're
lonely, that's the truth.
We can go a little bit together
& I'll show you
how I
found out my own Places."
My eyes flickered over to the Marques—
what will he make of it,
unjealous as he's said to be?
"Dont trouble your head about Rinaldo—
he's in his six-month retreat,
preparing a magical operation.
We will come to Palma together, yes,
& somewhat share?"
                    I agreed, almost
absentmindedly; I was watching So
with a new interest. She nudged me
under the table. "Magic, his way of it,
is old & of little value
until one has almost

56

outgrown one's native sexuality.
Time for that later.
What we're doing
is what Lull & Bruno & Leibnitz tried,
as much beyond magic
as electricity is beyond . . . well,
oxcarts." —And as dangerous?
"Isnt the Grail worth it?"
—That's how I talk about it, the chalice
filled with His perpetual blood,
hidden in my head.
"Not just the head. The head
is, how shall I say it,
filled with shit.
It is the dungheap
alchemists spoke of,
whence the pearl."
—No, Isabella, they meant more
& less than that.
"Granted. But grant me
that extension, or, better, that
*intention*, intensification of,
their meaning."

I allowed it. The boat moved.
We went to our separate cabins.
After some sleep, a steward
banged on my door.
Dark night on deck. I shivered
in the wind, still sleepy.
Her white garments fluttering she came,
the old Marques behind her. The three of us
went down a swung staircase,
stepped into a launch.
No moon at all.
When we were settled,

the launch, operated
by people I could not see
forward on the bridge,
moved off. The ship
behind us blended
soon enough into the dark.
Then nothing, till the sea
began to separate from the sky
& a dark shape where they joined,
a land in the place between.
"That's the island," she said,
"we're not exactly near Palma."
She said nothing else.
After a while
the Marques de So
as if talking to himself
murmured beside me
"At the beginning
of any magic
it is important, so very
important,
to buy a cock,
a cock
without haggling."

# 4

The first days of love are full of anger
but have no history.
This work,
that knowledge,
have no charts.
Take care of them,
be gentle.
Let them speak
without any graph
to guide
as if any
human thought
were labyrinth.

Ariadne.
A woman
interested in a stranger.
Her life
was corridors
led nowhere.
Theseus
led somewhere.
She led him.
Far off a beastly
kind of voice roared,
a monster —
her image
of the two of them
joined into one

being.
A maidenly thought,
false, impossible,
not even valuable
could it be won.
He roared.
He was older, & knew.
It didnt work out,
how could it.
He left her
on some island.
All her life
was haunted
by the notion
that a man & a woman
could walk one way.
Eventually
she followed her own thread
to the double nature.
A god.
I think she vanished
into the cosmic rift
between their natures
as the sun
poised a long time
between sea & sky
eventually goes down.

The true Labyrinth
is the Palace
of the Double Axe.
Two blades, separate,
wielded
by one haft.
That's the hope of it
& in that hope

maidens & young men
of ancienter Crete
delighted
to dance
their separate natures,
always
knowing the Third
alone could join them —
the bull they leapt.
Wine
poured out,
the thick gum
of poppy offered
to the goddess-with-two-hands,
holiest
because here.
The goddess is who worships her.
They went to sleep
in the same bodies,
the same love.
Above them
the sun set between the horns of the great bull.
Or rose there,
they were not particular
about their times,
they were not
afraid of the dark (of the sun)
(of the shadow)
(of a mistake).
But in Ariadne's time
the king came in
like seafog
& she fell in love
with the *way* somewhere,
with roads & the idea
of going them —

61

no island
needs a path.
All that's left
of Ariadne's
a patch of tweed
torn off her cloak,
her traveling clock
on an indifferent rock.
The rose
reminds itself of thorns.
The fragmentary lover
is left
with his catalogue of stimulations,
trumps
of his affections,
not sure of himself.
Mimulus
for timidity,
flower of the vine
for overconfidence.
The flowers
assort themselves
in the natural field;
the giant cultivars
are no good to him.
He has to go back
to find dense growth
of the wild flower
growing
where the world
wants it to grow.
What flower
bears his signature?
Poison ivy for
those afraid to touch?
And then someone wakes up

knife in hand
& history starts again
cheaping & changing
& paying debts
never dreamed of
in the sun's
contract with our flesh.
Think of the beautiful soldiers
riding white horses
to forgotten battles,
Lieutenant Legrand
as Baron Gros painted him,
steel-cuirassed, a flare
of scarlet round the steel,
his full thighs in white,
curve out of crotch, the manhood
so nicely revealed in male
costume of the time, white,
high boots, his steel-gilt helmet
under his arm, scarlet-dyed
ostrich plume atop.
Full-lipped teenager,
redblond norman hair,
dark eyes looking off
into the middle distance
seeing nothing.
Or nothing that touches him:
he will not live
to be between.
His chestnut mount, nose
turned down in the foretaste of death,
stands wellbred behind him.

A beautiful young man?
Certainly a beautiful uniform
but I'd know those eyes anywhere,

& for all their youthfulness
not call them beautiful.
They are too willing
to take advantage,
be taken advantage of.
Death our endless war
from which all others
are distractions.
Young men
are so easily distracted
(sigh of the old baroness).
O death
you work so little,
you are the laziest
most self-assured,
we will confute you
with wakefulness.
What we? I come to myself
on a bare hillside,
no more articulate companion
than a coyote (is it?)
down there
slinking off the path.
In that sense
I am alone.
The lady
who knows my mind
grows me a flower
I can understand
in the turns of my maze.
This flower
is called forgiveness,
Blake found it
beneath the dead vines
of all his self-denials,
plucked it, ate it

& learned to forgive
all those whose energies
had challenged his own
to corporeal love,
& to forgive himself
for not confronting
the tumult of his images,
a dream in the mind of a stranger.

Abandoning reward & revenge
the awakened one
cherishes only his alertness.
Dreams are dragon-snorts,
worth little, the beast
is an extension of his hoard,
its hostility
to whatever does not add to it.
All the pronouns
live in me.
Ariadne, withered on Naxos
among the fogs,
awaiting an identity,
is pregnant with herself.
Let me work hard
to keep her from falling
into the hands
of unmidwiving therapies
lest the new life
die out of her
& she take her place
in the ranks of the mature,
sailing her pretended orgasm
over the empty seas
she's been told
lead her to Theseus.
*Become* the labyrinth, Ariadne,

swallow your thread.
Immerse in that queendom
where the golden child is waiting,
seed of New Ariadne,
kernel it will take a Human Age
to grow.

I reach into my mind for you,
reach inside you
& display her,
here, needing no Hero.
A woman who is herself
steps up
from the murky shallows of the poem
& on proud hips walks away
from this & every
mythology
out into morning.

Do not turn
& condemn me
whose sleep
was your slavery,
do not kill me
because you have become your own.

5

The green water is combed
by naked bodies.
Pearl fishers or sporting lovers?
Both are meant.
A play of water
over the roses
from the hoses
is afternoon.
The rose
belongs to the sun.
Its thorn
is mine.
Crete
          is on my mind.
Taken back
into nevernever
where I can look at it
long enough
while the air
conditioner roars
& the radio sounds music
I cant put a name to.
The green water is sliced
by naked bodies,
sponge divers or escaping
lovers
weary of the island where they met?
Both are meant.
It is tropical, a lagoon,

hardly any wind
comes in off the sea.
It is passive,
propositional.
It teaches itself calmly
(reading from notes)
to anyone who looks down
from the beach-heads, from the red
cliffs
& has nothing better to do
than understand the sea.
(Understand me!)
It's that kind of day,
not too hot, a fog
rolling in, glints
of pale sunshine on the waters,
bathers, where they'd look at me strangely
if I said 'Forgiveness'
& keep going. Or keep sitting there
& expect me to be on my way.
All right. I got the message
by midnight: the world
will not end today.
The glint of the half moon
is quick on the naked swimmers
breaking water
near the falls, the wide
pool with algae at its banks
but clear & fast in the middle
where they turn
over & plunge again.
I'm superstitious,
I count them. I do not join them.
I do not want to swim.
Soon the river comes to the sea
& in the harbor

a big red boat is waiting with slack sails.
It has brought
x from y. It is a merchantman,
its owners
believe in movement. They move
along the coast under a fair wind.
They get here. They wait.
Men in dories
are unloading big vases & kettles —
are they the merchandise or just
containers? A subtle problem
that in three thousand years
will have created a talmud & a code of laws.
Right now, the only worry
is not to drop them
where the current is strong,
might carry
an amphora full of oil
far out to sea.
That would be no kind of fulfilment.

A grizzled blond man was beside me.
I turned & said: "I perceive
you are the crafty
Odysseus." "What makes you think so,"
he said. "Because of the graceful way
you dance those minuets of Lully.
Because of the snot
trembling under your nostril — you are
no stranger to affliction. Because
I recognize that massive ring,
two serpents each swallowing the
same gazelle. Pythons, I suppose?"
"Some kind of snake, who cares
to be more precise." "You're right,
it is that kind of day."

We were silent until he said
"That one's mine, but you can have
the redhead she's with, I have
enough trouble without Cro-Magnon
women." Generous of him I thought,
since the one he saved for himself
was thickwaisted & walked
ploddingly, while the one he planned for me
was taller by a head, very thin,
her small breasts moving slightly
while the breasts of the other
jounced like saddlebags.
"It takes all kinds," I said.
"Dont it just." "Are you Odysseus?"
"Call me Ulysses, it sounds better
in your uninstructed mouth."
"I beg your fucking pardon, there is no need
to be uncivil." "Call me what you like, then.
Virgil — somewhat on your order —
called me Ulixes, if I remember right."
"He was confused by earlier epigraphic
testimony, where X represented
an obsolete italiote sibilant, more like S."
He looked at me with wonder, looked away
& lit a menthol cigar. "Christ, another
Christian!"
    Meantime the girls
had made their way to the clifftop
not without panting. They came on,
& I was thinking that my prize
was not too pleased with me.
We'll make the best of it,
what more can we ever do.
Her name was Korinna, & she wrote verse,
some of it pretty good. At least
we had something in common — though that's the last

70

thing lovers ever should have.
They should only have themselves.
Ulysses interrupted: "Look,
what matters in a woman
is how she cooks & cleans, how much
attention she pays to you
when you're around. Dont go abstract
on her. Eat up, lie down, dont talk too much.
That's my advice to you."
Korinna & I looked at him with distaste —
another bond between us,
one more obstacle. We could now
so easily start to confuse
one another with notions of
complementarity, polarity, all my life.
The wind, listless as it was,
was astringent. I was fed up
with my usual ways.
                    "Korinna, we're
going to do what you want, whether you
want to or not." She smiled:
"I've met your kind before. Lazy,
lecherous, indifferent to choice.
Ulysses was right about one thing:
let's not talk too much. Be quiet
& I'll hang around till the boat goes."
We went off together, wandered
around the rocks, ate some sausages
she'd brought in her apron pocket.
She recited some of her work while I ate
three links to her one. I can never
get my songs by memory.
But I liked what she said.
We found a little hollow
& made love twice; the second
time she straddled me. We slept

a little while together,
our arms around, the grass
damp under us. I woke first,
a little more wind now.
Down in the harbor, the sailors
were chanting an ugly song
from Asia Minor. Ulysses
was snoring (apparently just
over the crest of our dell)
& his girl was cooking something
that smelled like liver & kidneys.
I extricated myself & got up,
disgusted, haunted by ugliness
here, at the beginning of things.
It was unspeakable. It was always
like this. Never different,
the ache
            of slow minds & dull weather,
everything too easy.
I resolved to take my life,
throwing myself down from the cliff
hoping to be broken on the rocks
before I drowned. I have always hated
drowning—almost did once;
it is supremely insipid,
like a year's boredom, year's stifling
plainness all jammed into five minutes,
fatal. I was looking down
when Korinna woke. "This is not
the beginning," she said, "this is just
another island of sleep. The beginning
is completely different. Believe me,
I knew it once. The way things are
is not how they are. You knew it once too,
I could tell it from your eyes
when we were fucking. Dont throw

yourself down.  There is nothing there,
neither rocks nor sea.  That is the worst
thing you could ever experience.  Take my word,
I have nothing else to give."

I wonder what I did then.  No memory
serves.  I came to myself in an open boat,
facing sternwards, watching a small wake
disappear fast on a calm dark sea.
A sneeze behind me.  It was Korinna,
naked as when we were on the hillside,
now shivering some.  I had a shirt on
I gave to her.  "I am surprised
to find us here, & you still with me."
"You cant get rid of a woman
easy as that."  "That's not
what I meant.  I mean I thought
that was fantasy, or this is fantasy,
or somehow then & now are disconnected,
different realities.  I'm glad you're with
me — you are very beautiful."
"My beauty is all you can use of me
but you're welcome to that.
Even now when it's cold, come near me."
"In a boat?"  "Why not?  It's very
nice in a boat.  You'll see."  I saw.
And we were warmer.  I wanted to ask her
who she was before I slept again.
Or who I was.  Or where we were.  Or why
I should think she could answer those.
Or why was I asking questions.  When it's sleep
it's like it's raining,
no part that isnt,
it all is.
        I slept, woke expecting to find
another reality.  It was the same.

This time she woke before me,
a warm morning. Nothing in sight.
"You should never have mentioned
Lully to Odysseus. Or made him smoke
a cigar. It's cheap." "I'm sorry,
but that's how it went down."
"Furthermore it's tasteless."
"I thought you were a poet, Korinna,
& poets are notorious
for bad taste."
"Not till your era."
"Besides, Odysseus called you
a Cro-Magnon woman, & spoke to me of Virgil.
Two directions of anachronism. Are you
Cro-Magnon?"
                    "I'm much earlier than Odysseus,
if that's any help.
I am one of the blonde witches
who lived in the Dordogne
just before the last glaciation.
We have very little purchase
on the people who came after, you folk,
you half-Neanderthals. Enough of our blood
(as you think of it, though it's hardly blood)
survives in you (especially you Celts
& other backwoods peoples) for you to see us
in dreams & psychoses, but most
in the fantasies of masturbators.
Every now & again, some fantasist
has a mind so intensely attractive to us
(not for reasons you could be proud of)
that we have no other way of making contact
but taking on flesh in the middle of his thought
& leading him out into the simple world.
It really is simple. We are one of the few
wrinkles in it. Here it is, flat as anything,

schematic, just barely
not abstract, a flat
ocean, a boat on it,
you & me in it,
talking. Good morning."
"Good morning, Korinna.
Where on the ocean are we?"
"Arent you surprised at what I told you?"
"I'm never surprised at the wisdom of women."
She got angry: "Dont compliment
me with generalities!"
"I'm sorry, I was being literal.
I didnt know about the Dordogne,
the interglacial. But I suspected
there must be somewhere
those women came from —
I remember them first
in my childhood sleeps,
I'd wake in the morning
expecting them still to be there,
between my bed & the window, or perched
on the orange-crate I dragged up one day
to store the few books I had,
I was five & must have known you then."
"Not me. There are many.
Succubae, an ugly word
for what we do. What we drain
is anger, not power, & a man
to whom we come
wakes
        ready for the world."
I had an odd feeling
I wanted to worship her,
grovel at her feet in the bilge
& offer her fish & octopus,
wreathe bullkelp on my cock

& rise to her, offering, offering,
sun & moon in my hands,
red sand, bananas, gold
snake bracelets, emeralds
I could pluck from my eyes,
raw fish, raw meat, a vein
ripped out of a bull still
spurting experienced dark blood.
"You have nothing to give me,"
she said, "except what you make up.
There are many forms of worship,
dont choose the easiest. The easiest
are spectacular gestures,
are for merchants & businessmen
in odd moments when they look up
from the women they buy & the stuff
they sell. The hardest
is what you do every day. Try that."
"Stop reading my mind," I said it
lightly, but she: "Your mind
is reading me." After that,
she went to sleep & left me
to watch where the boat went —
that was the whole of my task,
no rudder & no sail, no mast
to hang one on.
                     I put my forearm
on the gunwales & my head on my arm,
the sea was very green today
& as I watched it some opacity
seemed to sink out of the water away
till I was looking into a translucent
ocean, full of forms & movements
& uncertain reposes. The green
water was combed
by naked bodies,

divers going up & down, lovers
swimming with interlocked arms,
face to face, back to back,
moving very fast. As far down
as I could see, the water was busy
with levels & establishments,
people moving from condition to
condition, no infants, no old
people, many buildings moored in place,
seaflags & pennons, two armies moving
towards each other, passing over &
under, never meeting, bright
helmets & seaweedy shields,
they moved spirally, came to the center
their march compelled them to,
turned round & moved back, always
looking for the enemy
passing sometimes above
sometimes below them.
Some of the people moved
as if their floor went up & down,
others moved to my sense of it
more conventional, but wherever
anyone moved, the place
he moved in seemed his place,
his space & he was right for it.
Men were plowing down there,
some pulling, some guiding the coulter,
& as the plow furrowed the water
the water would heal again
but where the plow passed
young men & women leapt into being
& swam out at once
away from the groove.
In the whole ocean
no one but men & women, no fish,

no dolphins, but there were many
flowers & vines, weeds with great
golden bladders the women would ride.
I saw huge bubbles with men
riding in them & on them, a sport
it seemed to be to break them,
chase & be chased, sometimes
the passengers would vanish when
the bubble broke, then reappear
behind their pursuers & pursue.
The people close enough to me
for me to tell their faces
were familiar, I knew them
but couldnt handle their names,
reached & got none, no matter
if they laughed or frowned,
I could not name them.
                              Far down
some motion came towards me,
straight up, slowly, stately,
a procession it seemed to be,
a crowd of girls each carrying
a torch, & the torches
burned in the water; behind them
a white man & a black man
were yoked to a great chariot
which for all its size they drew
without effort. Two lovers
were standing in the chariot,
their eyes towards me, & for a time
I thought they were the monarchs
of this kingdom — then I could see
that they too were yoked
to what they rode on, & moved
& were moved in one motion. She
stood aside from him a little

& between them I could see a figure
clothed, the only one
in the whole sea
who wore clothes,
long dappled robe
concealing the sex.
This one began to
speak, from the mouth
the ripple of words
came towards me,
broke the green surface
& I heard them,
THE MIND BELONGS TO ITSELF.
Then I knew I was awake
& Korinna was talking.
"Do not watch too long.
The mind belongs to itself
until Adam begins to name
what he perceives. Then
Adam
must be destroyed. His first
death is in Abel.
His last death is in you.
Your weapon is Eve.
Know her
without her name.
She is naked to you
& with your will & work
the garden he defined
will flower again.
It is Infinity,
the secret
hidden in the heart of Time.
Awake, & take her."

The light was green.

I had kept the car in gear
all the while
now drove slowly
across the intersection,
did that twisty
right turn between the ranks
of cabs, pulled
into the first slot.
The bus
had been on time
& I had not.
She was waiting
in a black cape coat,
soft grey dress
with a silver
flower on her breast
sinuous, reminding me.
She ran to the car
before I had chance to get out,
her coat blowing out behind her.
We kissed, shyly,
in the way
such things are given,
a meaning
easily denied
by later fear.
But all my fear
was behind me.
She looked at me
almost tentative,
she meant
what she meant
but was
in gentleness
prepared
not to force

my meaning
on me.
I still had
a chance to die.
On the bridge
high
over the wide river
I greeted her
again, called her,
drove fast to get
home, set
my hand on her thigh
to show her
I had understood.

# 6

Morning
is not the sun.
Delbrück leaning forward
to quote Schiller,
*Das Talent reift in der Stille*,
of his own young manhood
when he'd learned
"as much as a man needs to"
& settled six years
where there was nothing going on —
& so became.
                    But it was a party
& Michael would trade all of Strauss
for two notes of *Wozzeck*, Lolli
was sorry about the lemon groves
dying all over, all over.
A girl in pink
hated the trailbikes
that brought foul emissions
to *her* mountains. "Exude" was what she
said. It was a party
& everywhere some sense
of backs against the wall.
Except the scientist;
"that was my best time"
his work
came to understanding.
He was released. From mountains
& the need to guard them, own them,

have opinions about them.
The girl who had just been
given a Ferrari
laughed hard at a joke about
grass. I walked aside (outside)
& fondled a lemon tree
most of the fruits still green,
one ripe, one gone to sleep
on the side, I pulled it off
& let it fall, sad
not to have brought Helen
one perfect one, covertly,
displayed from my pocket.
But I wouldnt
take the one ripe lemon on a tree.
I went back inside, the dog
did not bark, the maid
did not turn around from the sink,
I had mopped my brow
with the linen napkin, had cooled
outside & come back in
as if I were no one, nothing
happened, no te conoce
. . . hormigas de su casa.
It was the same, but different.
The girl in pink
looked more than ever
like a Renoir, widefaced,
softbottomed, the splay
of plump thighs on the rug,
the vermouth in the glass
caught some of her light.
The mood. If light's a mood
we are its minions,
are mastered by it, can I fight
free of color? Will I wind up

blind? Without my glasses
I know the world only by color,
what victim I. I had been
outside, among the regular
hedgerows, what looked like a
formal garden away over the last,
fading in the dim light out of
discriminable form. I came back in,
dessert was on the buffet,
berries in papaya halves, cookies
& dried fruits. The cookies
stuck together by their chocolate
bottoms. Black bottom. Pink
bottom, to be able to be
a simple sensualist, lick the Renoir
like raspberry ice
& not to have a thought in my
head about it. Not a word.
*Earlier today*
*you climbed the pale barked*
*fig tree, gathered figs*
*ripe & almost,*
*let them fall*
*into my cupped hands.*
I missed some, & those
dropped into the ivy,
so tender that the three foot
fall bashed them open,
earth & leafmold stuck,
I brushed a few off & ate
anyhow, very sweet, the violent
surprising inner red
(spread thighs), ancient fruit.
Lemon groves.
I should have brought Lolli out
maybe & shown her the lemon tree,

but it would not have mattered,
her loss was so personal
that any objective tree
would be no evidence
for joy, no writ of gaudeamus.
I should have brought Michael out
& sung Apollo's monologue
*Jeden heiligen Morgen* (my voice
would not rise to it,
but in all this
suppositious, what's a
tessitura among friends?)
where the god
summons up,
as Sun,
his specific power
to change girls into trees
or deliver women
from the death of groves.
I worry about him, Apollo,
lest he pluck
the one ripe lemon
from the tree.
But Lolli would have grieved
& Michael gone on
cherishing "that most perfect
wedding of text & music,"
as we are all, haunted,
by, a, perfection, it,
is, not, possible, to,
make, in, any, work, but,
only, in, the body of
a flowing.
       No word
says it all.
I believe her

body
a little
but Renoir stinks.
Bach cantata,
the tenor is good
I mean I can believe
the words in his mouth
naturally sung.
Tenor — the sustained
or sustaining melody,
& he who sings it.
Would I have grieved
at the dead tree?
The party
goes on,
but our powers
mature in quiet,
ripen
in the silence of the tree.
What have I come
back in upon?
Annette & David
hold this house
in their hands,
we move
within their grooves,
they are so used to us
whoever we are
that their lives
persuade us
how to move.
There are paths
through the house.
She says "telluric,"
there is a power
of earth in the bone

of her face, there is earth
in the way it goes, here,
no one
daring to hope aloud,
earth I tracked in
from mucking around
in the garden,
I see it on the white
sole of my shoe,
it is an edge
between my composure
& the rug,
we drink cappuccino
from tiny cups.
I do not spill mine
(you have to warn me once),
I do not crush
this eggshell Chance
between my fingers
(as I would not be
crushed
between her thighs,
Tykhê, Chance, strange
girl on the edge of
things?). I relent.
What is this edge
between house then & house
now?
        It is not George MacDonald's
home is what
you can enter & leave.
I come in
from the cool earth air,
the garden
in midOctober,
I do not live here,

& I did
find a fruit outside,
this golden
(why is silence
golden? I had to know
when I was a child,
I grew it then, drew on it,
drew it on
& wore it a long time,
good wool, cut
from a healthy chimera,
spun by Mother Eve,
in an off-moment
stained with her
menstrual blood, a seamless
robe, a silence)
this golden yellow
kernel, this silence
I carried in with me
to hear
(almost as soon
as I sat down)
Das Talent
reift in der Stille
& I cannot show you, Helen,
what I found
except later, always
so much later
when the party's over
& all the people gone
home decently,
forgetting, letting
the whole thing slip
decently, then I come in
filled with my report
of what I was really saying

while I was talking constantly,
what I felt & who it was
I begin now to remember,
coming in with all that
as if to prove
the fruit I carried
was perfect, now breaking it open,
irrevocable,
to share it with you.

# 7

First rain
in weeks, to hear that
trickle & crackle
& not at first know
what it was, then going
out & standing in it
to remind. This morning at ten
the streets look damp, the grass
& ivy wet, my left foot
on the way to the mail
brushes the little ferny bush,
gets wet. And the sky
is piled with every kind of cloud,
grey humping over San Gabriel,
black swarm on La Cañada.
Down there the clouds thin to fog
over Los Angeles, far down
a patch of sunlight on them,
a clump of tall buildings, white
in all the grey surround.
Remind.
      To call my mind back
into the senses
& to the sense of things
as they are
in themselves.
A philosophic program
(maybe), but not a formal
intention.

Only (& everywhere)
the intention towards Form.

34 N 12   118 W 07′40″
called Poppyfields
because for years
& then they came
& dreamed
houses on the hill.
Not the true
poppy of opium
but that less somnolent
orange flower of the west,
simple calix, wind-filled,
here recently
enough for a color
snapshot of the fields
verging down
towards Pasadena
signed with all the days of sun,
mountains over us
reverberatory furnace,
banking the heatshot
down on us again.
But the grey day
is its own opium,
allows a concentration
clearer than alkaloid,
a cool wind nurtures
what I suppose.
The orders
are elaborate;
the strings are tuned.
Inside every image
another is visible.
In the nucleus

the whole world
reposes
on a tantric
vivid leaf.

The wind
blows an empty paper bag,
not empty any more.
Shut my mouth.
*Until this wreath*
*blossoms*
with the bitter
white flowers of irony,
healing mistletoe
of analysis,
I will be silenced
by the ease of life.

       Leap
for the rope
at certain hours swung
down from the stars
into the dungeon.
It may not be hard to climb,
but the first leap
has to be made, no one
can help there, to leap
straight up
& hold on hard
if anything finds its
way into your hands.
How to live
to be ready for that.

The Hero
begins his research

into the matter of dark woods.
It will lead him
to an act
he will confuse with himself.
Then he must suffer
his appetite to know
*die Menschen und Weibchen*
*im grünen Gefild',*
the people of earth
in all their gaiety
on the green fields.

The Hero
must bring
a syntax
elaborated
a year & a day
far from all women
but inside one
under Mount Venus
where the sun
goes down
to be spoken
in his mouth.
His is the syntax
& the birds
complete.
Hence the hero
must be guileless,
fatuous,
a copious flow
of syntactic patterns
commodious
of sense. The birds
stick the lexemes in,
the words I mean;

they build the nest
from what they find.
His empty head
is gracious to receive.

His search
digs in his senses,
responses. The clue
is hidden there
(dragon nature; man
nature; structure of gold,
purpose of rivers;
structural capacity
of engine
              to function,
functional capacity
to move him
                —the Chariot,
Arjuna seductive
over the horses)
& let him be moved
by what he finds
in him to move.
The clue is there
no trumpet
to lead to it, no bird
to hunt it down.
Sun our falcon
at the top of the sky
hunts us all down
into our time
(comes out now, 2:57,
blinding by contrast
on the white garden wall)
to coax him to learn
(every Hero must)

the language of birds.
In this laboratory
where they talk true
latino, chitter
like china in faraway
kitchens, blither,
make melody,
tone rows, crisscross,
matrices confused,
grids broken, wilful,
wilful, messiah's
name & birthplace
garbled, numbers tweet,
eeny miny
lethera pethera pump,
sex, Sheba, late nine
moon,
birthplace,
marketplace, Balkis,
seas, marrows, clams,
ganoids, grant mes,
nine moons all at
sixes & sevens, placenta,
Artemis, Astarte,
Astartemis, give us,
yield, yield our yield
all at once, keep
(keép keep, keép keep)
nothing,
hold nothing back.

# 8

What I've lost of you
I've had to lose —
& however you sense the loss
you are sealed
in this work.
And there's the house I mean
to make in any image
or any worked thing,
a hollow place
to take us in — maybe
not for long, but that
in everything
there be a space for us —
as the hallows
in all religions
seem to be *bundle*,
*cup*, *enclosure*,
the sealed garden
of the most secular
mind
      in the core whereof
transpires in all her
holiness & dread
the necessary Rose.

I conceive my skull
patient
beneath & between

my desires & their
named destinations,
skull sturdy, skull
skilful to be unnoticed,
the ultimate cave.
And am I talking there now
or is some magic left
in rain & air
that these fabrics
may be worn some day
by a living body
in what I read as beauty
advancing
clean of me & almost
of herself, existential
woman?
I want to fuck you
& my skull inclines.
This "you"
is more general
than the day allows —
but I must suffer my will
to be single.
There is only one Sun!
— & It comes out now
flaming its way
into my mind
not a minute too soon.
Loom of skull
through my time-
begotten skin
be less oppressive now,
lighten
in the accomplishment —
everything done
releases me.

The Nurse speaks:
You have reached me now
        in time,
it is all right now, •
        now
you will not die —
        my business
is not with living & dying
but proposing
                your task:
receive
    all the voices, hear them
& predict,
            wisdom
        is just a leaf
    of a holier earthier tree,
wood of your wood,
                        dense
matter of,
        let me hear,
it could have been song.


And so to the skull,
inside it
the witnesses live,
agents from the burning
world
who come to set fire.
The intricacies,
Christ the folds
of this world
we are supposed to share!
And all my sense
follows the contours,
accepts the hill.

The box of bluetip matches.
The wind chimes
of strung dentalium shells.
The ivy. Smell of burnt meat
the smell of rain.
The loaf of bread,
a knife
beside it, Isaac slain,
Christ slain, Mohammed
talking to the sun.
The friends who came to me
in the persuasion of love,
the friends I failed
the friends who failed me:
they do not balance
with an orange, one
with heavy rind still
green around the stem.
The peppermill, the manual
of counterpoint, Couperin's
Tenebrae for Maundy Thursday,
the hose the watering can
the broom. The bone.
The fountain pen.

                    That image
stands up now
from the *Poliphilo*,
how the lover
was made to follow
a woman with long red hair
who was naked, & as she went
before him up the green
made shift to hold
her long hair upon her arm
to show him her behind, & how,

his eyes on that,
he found himself conducted
to a fountain of instruction
where he learned his Beloved
was one & many
& some of her was masked
with faces not for him —
but many of her voices
spoke to him;
with those he had
like any lover
rapturously
to make do —
all that
to be at home
in her garden.
Was it hers?
But all these voices
then & now
hum in his head,
he is baffled
by clarity.
He needs the pencil
& the loaf of bread.
The chair. The vine.
The two-ring stove.
The banana. License
plate, the card
in his pocket
with his name on it.
A snapshot of his love
looking one way long ago
but he sees her
all different ways.
He needs the rope
the hose the bucket the brush

the shoe the cigarette
the highway map the lightswitch
the window all the time.
He prays to the door
that it open.
He prays to the night
that it engage him
within its operations.
He prays to his knees
that they not
be submissive. He holds
a trowel in his hands
& prays to the angels of
architecture. The angels
of the day hours
& the night hours
are known to him by name.
He counts nothing.
The trees
are safe from him.
He prays to the stove
that it boil a living water,
he prays to the water
that it be willing
to bear heat. He prays
to the rain to fall always,
wiping away his shame
& contentment. The trowel
rusts. The saucer
fills up with rain.
He imagines himself
a royal freemason
praying all night
for revolution. He stands
on the tip of his shoelace.
When he moves

he moves heavily,
accepting the direction
he imagines
the ground demands.
He prays to the bridge
that it may bring him to her
but does not cross it.
He prays the falcon
to carry his message,
a letter he will not write.
He prays to time
that its teeth be clement,
that time should become
space & he be free
within it, all that distance
& no need to travel it,
distance as positive,
to live in, live, he prays
to his heart to accept the world
& to the world
that it be interesting
to the end. Watching
her buttocks
sway up the gentle
lift of the garden
he needs the flower
& the glass full of
polarized light,
he accepts the woman
who leads him
as his beloved,
he is wrong & right.
He calls her the World
& worships her
praying to Nothing
that he be left

free of distraction
& so be able to
center
on what he imagines
to be happening.
Clearly, he needs the trowel,
charcoal, brick,
stovepipe, the trowel,
soft shoes, penpoints,
flowerpots plain & painted,
deserts, highways,
fingernails. He needs
the ruined cathedral. The trowel.
The bus. The pocket
full of money & two stones.
Agates & an ocean
to wash them in. He needs
to do what he's doing.
He follows her
into the only direction.
The door he disdained
opens.


The nursemaid
sits at the table
in the kitchen
smoking cigarettes.
Her lipstick
is very red.
She smiles at me
& breathes out
a long plume of smoke
towards me.
It smells wonderful,
I feel the smell of it

down below my belly
along with the shape
of her mouth, her
smile. She has friends
with her, two women
one her sister. They
smoke too, taking
cigarettes from a dark
green pack. They have red
mouths, they also
smile at me. I am happy
at last. What I feel
stays with me for years,
I come back
to that moment
& know it is me.
The women, even the older,
I learn long after
are really only girls.
My maid (it is told me)
is young—not twenty yet.
The three of them
are smiling at me, I must
have said something.
They are not working,
they are sitting
in my mother's kitchen
doing nothing. It feels
daring to do this, it feels
exciting, I am on their
side. Let me sit here.
I dont know how old I am,
still need her help
in the toilet. I feel
like three. In the bathroom
off the kitchen

she wipes me clean, my face
is pressed against her
belly, my hands for balance
hold onto her thighs
while I crouch forward.
Her thighs my balance.
But now I am at the table
looking up at the three of them
in turn, all smoking,
all with red mouths. I say
nothing. My penis
(my witness) is swollen
& I am at peace. Never
to end.
The nursemaid
sits in the kitchen
smoking cigarettes.
Lucky Strike, green.
Her lips are very red.
In that moment
I have lost my age.
I am there still.
A giant baby
I stare with wonder
up at the mouths of women,
at peace to smell
the breath from their lips,
rich smell of the smoke
after it has passed
through their bodies
& comes out again,
breathed, a blue plume,
I see their words
breathed, the mist
takes me into itself
& I can talk with them.

A table with four sides,
a child at one
& a woman at each other,
their breaths, the touch
of their hands, sweet
breath breathed on me,
they are
extraordinary,
it is the kitchen
of my house
but only this once,
my nursemaid
& her friends
stealing the time,
her skin is so soft,
she talks
over my head,
her brown hair
veils my face
when she bends
to help me
dress or undress,
her hands are soft
wherever they touch me,
I learn to talk,
I say something
that makes the three
women smile.
I collect their smiles,
their smell, their breaths,
her pale body
when I watched her bathing —
there is peace for me
in being there,
the beautiful Time
they squander

in being beautiful,
I've got to say something
that will make them
let me go on
sitting at the ivory table
hearing them, feeling
them, taking them in.
Something
so that when it counted
halfway across my life
they would turn
in time
to take me in.
That I could become
the smoke they breathe,
& the violent touch
inside them
that would bring
also those soft smiles
& faraway looks,
their half-open red
mouths
also would take me.
These were the nurses,
not concerned
with giving birth,
not with the propagation
of a species
it was no work of theirs
to understand,
but to take
what life
was given!
into their incredible hands
& use
all their mouths

to foster
in delight & demonstration
the use of time
to the secret work
I felt then growing
in their neglect
of the clock,
to tear the living body free
from the gears of labor
& sit beside it,
flesh with flesh
& welcome each life
to the breath
inside it
& little by little
lead it
(breath by breath)
to speak
itself
into the eternal air.

# 9

Sonata in A<sup>b</sup>, op. 110
*Essay on Form*

Sonata in A$^b$, op. 110
*Essay on Form*

A mile above us
it was snowing.
Even down here
a sweater was good,
this old green one
from my sister,
big hole
under right arm,
not moth, just wear.
The calm of it,
to wear some clothes
so long they fall away —
nothing
that is not casual,
that does not
fall.
La Vérité
is day by day.

I want to say a language
the way lovers learn,
names of their parts first,
shaky on rules.
The world is all exceptions,
runes
so slow
to carve in,
                words

slower than honey dripping,
appearing no faster than
a leaf dries after the rain —
so song is possible
                              (division
of tones over time,
stepwise)
                    —if Time
were all at once,
no melody.
Go slow.
Nothing amounts to much
except in time.
I mean go slow.
I mean to make
love to you too.
If that's permitted.
If not,
            well, under some bridge.
The arches. If I cant have you,
I'll wait for your daughter —
moving
            with the inertia
of all things,
                    slow as a day,
irresistable.
                    Singleness
lies in the intention
to embrace.

The ultimate
is intimate.
I learned that
from my chastity,
long years festering
in virginity,

at thirteen to guess
the dimensions I shared
with a world, the fact
of loss
                would never be made up.
But the shape of love
like the loom of morning
could cast before it
a light on the shapes of things
made *realer* by the goal
towards which it & I & all
hopeful things were moving.
To make love.
The pain was real,
& warps me still —
but that was realer,
everything
                led to you.
The connection
is too delicate
to stress.
                Let me hide
it in civility:
real, realer?
what kind of words
are those,
                the bee knows
how real the rose.
The physical world
yields its unity
to our metaphysical fact:
*To listen*
*when it does not speak.*
To determine
the exact distance
between any word & any other

111

& by skill to map
the landscape between.
Then coax the word to speak.
Melody
especially when it grieves
(arioso dolente)
takes your hand.
Leads you
willing or unwilling
to the pine-lit
wedding chamber,
you are married
to the fact of it,
the light goes out
on all you've felt
or failed to feel.
Grief
          is the distance
between loves
                    sometimes stepwise,
sometimes reversing
its course
as when we move close
& grief is the cave
our present joy
lights up,
          go slow,
grief is distance,
even the miles we traveled
to be in bed together
ache under us.
Just this once
not to be caught
in statement or story,
but to flow
justly

over the contours
of your body
in the liberty of light.

Truth is a day,
& every day.
Refute that
& be wiser
than your eyes,
& sorry.
I want to take your time,
linger
is the shape of it,
an hour
is to go through.
Gate after gate.
That is what the form of words
(forming a place for words)
lets in,
       & what the Matter is
of our work,
to let the time
speak itself through.
Sometimes
we've been making love so long
we almost forget
we're doing anything,
& then an acceleration
begins in my throat
to find some word
shaped like what it is
to be me in you,
that might answer
all the subtle
information
to which your body

all this while
subjects me,
learning
while my heart & breath
hunt for the word
(it must sound like you)
& when I look at your eyes
sometimes open
the humid fire
so far below
increases
& I am urgent to say
so that from an immense distance
further than any grief
a word begins to travel
through me, I can hardly
understand it, I am not even
interested in it, it approaches,
I want to brush it away,
I will not submit
to its definition, but its will
seduces mine, it has your
name on it but
is not yet your name,
I hold you tighter now
& the word catches fire,
burns me, the smoke
conceals its sound, the fire
seems more like your fire,
there is affinity, a rime
aching to sound, its road
begins to open, my gates
burned down & nothing but
gates everywhere opening,
I know what the word must be,
its simplicity

has tricked me again,
I struggle
to resist
the ease of it,
it has come
from everywhere I am
& will not be refused,
even, there begins
to be no longer any
part of me that knows
how to refuse,
I look at your closed eyes
& know
there's no hope anywhere,
what you are doing
being
now
        is irresistable,
you declare a fire & a hollow
& a world
                the precise shape
of what must come
now
        leaping to fill it
& louder than I could
ever have imagined
it suddenly speaks.

# 10

"However far I get this time,
when I have to fall back
I will do so

       master
of some fraction of a mountain.
On that I can exercise my sense
of size, can plan ahead, & more
than those: I will have declared
at least that, it will be done,
however far I fall short, I can
begin from there the next time."

His language was fluent & awkward,
he moved that way too, each word
jerking out like a third arm
as he moved over the gentle meadow
at the foot of the mountain.
I was walking with him
to his base camp, set modestly
at the first level spot on the trail.
I hate to talk while walking
so I said nothing, grunted
in what sounded like agreement.
A woman was with us, a friend of his
who was quiet, rangy, kept
walking ahead & falling back.
She carried nothing, & his slowness
seemed to annoy her.
She interested me more than the mountain.

116

We climbed for an hour
then leveled out
at the shack
he had built for him
five years ago when he began.
His fancy was to roof it
with lopped boughs of pine —
but wisely these were set
over a plain pitched
tarpaper roof. I dumped my pack
eagerly — provisions for his camp
I had offered to carry.
The girl started a fire
between two stones
set there for that,
using char from the last fire
& heaping some roof boughs
on it to make flame —
she just reached up & yanked
as many as she wanted loose.
He seemed to disapprove,
but said nothing. When the fire
was good, he brought a big
aluminum pot up from the spring
& set it to boil. "Mountain soup,"
he said, & dumped some cornmeal in,
an old dried onion, a strip
of jerky, some pine gum, a clot
of salt from the damp cardboard box
kept in the shack. "Bears
have been here recently," she said.
While the stuff was cooking
I stood on a firm rock outcrop
over the talus slope
that dropped back to where,
almost exactly, we had started.

I could see my car on the grass
at the end of the pebble road
on the other side of the
lake at the end of the wash.
The car was good to see,
a comfort.  I understood
the world it moved in, even
if I never did exactly know
what made it go.  The soup
began to give off smell now.
The girl came over & said
she was surprised to find me
looking backwards.  I said I liked
heights very much & she agreed.
I wished that it was she
who was making the soup.  She smiled
but said nothing else.  How long
have you known him, I asked.
She said he was an old friend
of her mother's, she had known him
since her childhood, always
filled with fun but now
demonstrably getting old.
When he'd asked her to come along
there had come unbidden
into her mind the memory
of a shiny cast-iron coach & four
brightly painted, with white horses,
he'd given her when she was about
six, for no particular reason.
She was very pleased with it still,
especially that it was not a doll.
She guessed she owed him her company
at least on the trail.  She agreed
to come up to camp, & there decide
after a day or so whether to climb

on further — she didnt much like
climbing, & once had a bad fall
from a real horse on a mountainside —
mountains were rough on horses.
I asked her what she did with
herself when she wasnt on horses
or mountains. She looked at me coldly
& then saw I really wasnt
being disrespectful. She was a chemist,
she said, working on her doctorate.
On the word 'chemist' she had looked at me
with a pause & an innocence, as if in hope
it would mean something to me — it did,
but not much. All I know about it,
I confessed, ends in the fifteenth century.
She said she hated antiques of any kind,
was born into her time & meant
to find the best of her time
& not compromise with the past. Here
we were in agreement, & I assured her so
at length. It was the beginnings
of a conversation. We had gotten
to the evils of Nostalgia when
he called out the soup was done.
We assembled at the pot & he
insisted on saying grace, in Hebrew,
while she ladled into our bowls
with a tin cup. She had some dried
apricots in a bag in her coat pocket,
she produced them & we shared.
They were better than the soup
but the soup wasnt bad. It had boiled
down & thickened well, salt
a little heavy. She boiled water
for coffee, not much of it, instant,
& he laced the cups with local

brandy from his flask, which he
then refilled from a bottle tucked
under the bedframe in the shack.
Black instant coffee, terrible,
but it got the cornmeal out of my teeth.
After we'd eaten he announced
he planned to start up right then.
"No sense to put it off. I'll start now
with still a few hours of daylight.
That means the first day climb
not too long, & I'll sleep better
knowing that I'm really on the way.
I know all that part of the mountain.
What I'm anxious for is what I do
not know — *that* mountain." He told her
she'd have to make up her mind.
She answered that she'd stay, here,
overnight, in case he needed her,
then, in the morning, go down
the mountain if he hadnt come back.
I said I'd stay with her — but
it had never been an issue that
I would attempt the real climb
of course. He saddled himself up
like a mule, all smiles, puffing
a lot but not really out of breath.
He rubbed the toecaps of his heavy
hiking shoes with a plantain leaf:
"It goes better," he said. And then
smiling he took off up the trail
puffing & whistling no sort of tune.
We watched him as long as he was in
sight, then turned to each other,
suddenly alone on the center of a
stage — embarrassment, we having
no present reason to be together.

I guessed aloud he had left so abruptly
to spare her a long time of having to decide.
She talked about her work, & I got on
as she feared to early chemistry,
the arabs, the 'mystical nomansland'
she thought it was — I agreed. We lack
the sources, & lack the sense of work
we'd need if we had them. That ended
that. We talked about Bergmann,
& I couldnt help getting excited
all over again about Gunnel Lindblom.
"But she's only an actress. I thought
we were talking about a work
of art!" I explained that Lindblom
was a presence, a numen exchanged
between the light of the film
& the dark of my mind. She is the most
woman I've ever seen on the screen,
I said. That is irrelevant, she said.
Music was no better; she ranged
from Joni Mitchell to baroque, not
very far. I grunted that hers
was graduate school taste. That won
a few minutes of hurt silence. I was
ashamed of having been so accurate.
She refrained from explaining
how I showed my age. Even on civil
rights we had no agreement,
she believing the blacks could act
independently & I supposing that only
if all people acted could the system
be changed. Broken. It was dusk
& she made more coffee, this time
measuring more into the cup. It was
better. She got the brandy bottle
from the camp; we decided

we could use half of what was left.
When we looked up from the fire
we were surprised to find it dark.
Full night. By now he must have
camped up there. We walked out
to the cliff top & looked back
up the mountain, wondering if
we could see his fire. We saw nothing.
She wondered if there would be bears
& it began to get clearly colder.
I went off into the trees to piss,
came back to the fire & she was gone.
I shivered over it a while, rubbed hands above it
till she came out of the woods
behind the shack. She pulled some
branches down & tossed them on, blew
into the embers & for a little while
we had a comforting blaze. We huddled
together & I held her close, warmer
now & not much to be said. We were quiet.
Once I heard what I thought was singing
far up above us. It sounded operatic
coming out of the night that way,
sentimental. "That would be just like him,"
she said, but didnt hear it herself.
We went into the shack & crawled into
the narrow single bed, piled everything on,
my jacket, her coat. It was too cold
to undress.
               Let us be
together, I whispered,
now, we will be warm enough,
nature will take care of us. She turned
her body away from me a little,
"I cant, I couldnt fuck with you
while he's up there on the mountain.

122

Try to understand, I couldnt,
with him alone on the mountain."
To be agreeable, I let her be,
but held her to keep us both warm.
After a while I forgave her.
I was asleep sooner than I could have
imagined. When we woke in the morning
we saw it had snowed. Here & there
some patches of it were still left
evaporating off in the hot sun.

# 11

*The grace that comes*
*to tolerate*
*each effort, the grace*
*to go on.*

*Death's eyes*
*greenly shining*
*are a smile*
*that draws.*

*The sense of death*
*is what I hold to*
*to begin to move.*
*To go on.*

*And the Maiden,*
*who has always*
*belonged to death,*
*the Kore, the*
*Girl*
*on her travels*
*below,*
*who goes with him,*
*she is the same*
*who beckons to me.*

The Hero
dark between his ears,
his labors

begin on the other
side of despair.
He wears the skin
of the Lion
ate him,
he carries as club
the tree
that crushed him down;
his intestines
are that Snake
who sucked his spiritual
semen
        down
into the circle of the earth
from beyond the Zodiac
it is the duty
of that Snake to guard.
The Hero
sweeps the shitty
floors of his mind.
The gods
are against him,
every one.
But their daughters
encourage him, he calls
one of them his mother
because she was the first
pair of tits he saw.
His labors
go on & on.  His meat
roasts on skewers,
he eats it
half-cooked, he knows
he has drunk
because his thirst is gone.
He moves too fast

to notice what he's doing.
*How precious*
*& how rare*
*human life is,*
*to be reborn a man*
*holding a conscious*
*chance,*
        he sings that,
holding the hope,
a chance
of conscious life.
His feet
keep getting in his way.
He stumbles
over no obstacle, he falls.
He moves on
to the next town.
He finds
that men respect him.
He doesnt like
that kind of town
but what is he
going to do? He likes
the gravy on the tough
meat, somebody
cooks it for him, a girl
brings it, it is a plate
covered with meat & potatoes
covered with brown thick
gravy. His teeth hurt.
A coke gets the meat down
but makes the teeth hurt worse.
The bread is so gentle,
he soaks the gravy up, wipes
the plate clean, the bread
is so kindly he almost cries,

*o soft bread.* He gives
the girl a dollar. She stands
still, not touching it.
He adds another dollar.
She goes away. He wants
to be in the street, he's in
the street, bread on his mind,
he stands on the curb.
Not many cars go by.
Plenty of money.
A little boy
is watching him
so he begins to move
down the street
facing the sun,
crosses to the shade,
goes around the corner.
Gas station.
A blue car
with chalky white top,
cloth, he could
enjoy riding in that,
car with a hat,
the coke grumbles
in his belly, he belches.
There must
be somewhere to go.
He asks the mechanic
how much is the car.
The man says some money
he doesnt understand.
The sun has come
around the corner too,
he has to begin
to move again,
it would be so nice

to sit still.
A bench, green slats of
wood.  A new corner.
He sits on the bench,
almost
he can begin to think.
A bus
stops at his feet,
door already open.
The driver
looks at him.
He gets in
with a dollar,
the driver puts
coins in his hand.
He sits behind the driver,
the bus goes.
It is good to sit down.
People get on the bus,
seats are filling up,
he prays that a woman
will sit beside him.
It is a little boy
who sits down. A friend
of his across the aisle,
they make a lot of noise
till the driver
shuts them up. Soon
they get off, the bus
empties out. They come
to the end of the line,
a corner
like where he started.
He gets off
& walks again
away from the sun,

is afraid
that's a mistake
turns
& faces it,
moves toward it,
allowing it to lead
him along.
He keeps walking
an hour,
the streets are empty,
edge of town.
The sun
is going down.
He walks
confident
that there is nothing
else for him to do.
It is a road now
simply, between fields
maybe planted, nothing
coming up yet
for him to tell.
He wonders
what it will be.
From behind him
a truck comes,
slows beside him,
stops.
Somebody in the cab
asks if he needs
a ride.
He guesses so, gets in.
He tries to think
of something to say.
The driver
doesnt care, doesnt

say anything either.
They drive
while it gets dark.
The headlights are on
& he doesnt understand.
He thinks about everything
simple as they are,
cones of light
sticking out, blurring
into what they show.
It's nice to be riding
he says. The driver
smiles at him.
Need a job? I guess so.
Know anything
about cows?
Somewhere
he had heard this line before,
he remembers
the big slow warm bodies
how hard it was
to get them to move.
A little bit, I guess.
I need a man
cause my brother's sick,
you'd have a nice
place to sleep & good food,
plenty of it. That sounds
fine. Job'll only last
till he's better, a hernia,
doctor told him
to take it easy a month
after the operation.
The truck
turned off the road
down onto dirt,

scrub all sides,
nothing big.
He wanted to get away,
it sounded familiar,
a cliché,
only one way
it could end, he didnt
know what it was
but it kept happening
before, the land
so flat & nowhere
to go. The man
sounded nice, he was
tired, they could help
each other out.
How can he help me?
he thought. He was
beginning to think.
They passed through
a gate.
This is our place
the driver said
but they kept moving
over the same land.
He wished
the lights would go out
the moon was there
beyond some buildings
just risen.
The truck stopped.
This'll be yours
the driver said
& got down to show him
how to get into the
cabin, three bunks,
a table & stove,

some chairs. Wash up
out back, then come over
to the house. The truck
went on, he watched
the red tail lights move
not far, a few hundred
yards, to a big house.
He lay down then
on the bunk
closest to the window,
got up & got undressed,
lay down again.
Got up after a while
& went out
to the pumphouse,
splashed water all
over him, went back
& combed his hair,
got back
into his clothes,
combed his hair again,
sat on the bunk.
What was this? What was
this going to be?
He looked at the floorboards
moving off west
as he had been
all day,
            he wondered
would he get there?
And *there* was the first
time he remembered it.
But the memory slipped.
He went over & sat
at the table. Ashtray
from tunafish can, a groove

bent in the side.
No butts in it. He had some.
He lit one,
put the match in the can.
Time to go.
He walked out, hoping
the latch would hold,
hoping it would not lock
& keep him out.
By moonlight
he found the right way,
followed the truck ruts
to the truck itself,
knocked on the door
where the house was brightest.
Come on in, it was
the big kitchen, a huge
plastic table with a littler
wooden one shoved up
against one end, plastic
tablecloths, a lot of plates,
big heap of bread.
The driver was the boss,
a rancher. His wife. The wife
of the sick man
who was not here, he was
in Denver, getting over it.
The rancher's three sons,
too young to do much work.
The daughter of the sick man,
about sixteen. An old man
who was help like him.
They sat at the table, big
enough for him to find a seat
without their bothering
to make room for him. He sat

as near to the bread as he could.
Off in the corner
the tv was running,
he watched it
since it was easy to do.
It was the news.
The temperature in Casper,
in Cheyenne. *I know
where I am.* It was an ad
for macaroni. That's
what they were eating,
macaroni & cheese, with
pieces of frankfurter in it,
he liked it, he had four
pieces of bread & some milk.
Lots of salt. Pretty nice food,
he said, & smiled at them.
Long time since I've had any
real family food. The girl
wanted to know what he did
but her mother said
Cant you see he's shy? let
the man alone to eat.
He smiled at the girl.
At her mother. He took
another piece of bread
& mopped up the cheesy
sauce on his plate.
He felt very sad, soft
again, like the bread,
like a woman somewhere
was sick, like somebody
was losing something
he never really had
in the first place, dumb
as a brave smile. The tv

was showing Lucy
& he looked away from it,
there was too much laughing
& he never understood.
The rancher was watching it,
& his wife. The three kids
were playing with a cardboard
airplane cut from a cereal
box. He watched that instead.
The biggest one had it in hand
but the littlest one knew
where a rubberband was.
The middle one just watched.
They made the plane fly,
it crashed
into the macaroni,
then went all across the room
behind the tv. Their mother
took it away
& they went out
into another room
while the grown-ups
had coffee & cake.
They had their cake
this afternoon
the wife of the sick man
explained. I hope your
husband
gets better soon, he said.
I hope so too,
Juney misses her daddy.
The girl blushed
& he pretended
not to see her.
He ate more bread
while the cake

was being cut.
You sure like bread
Juney said. He smiled & said
it's good for you.
The cake was coffeecake
& very good.
He helped them clean up,
liking to do it
& liking to help.
The rancher
the two women & the girl
played cards.
Breakfast at five
the rancher said.
So he thanked them
& said goodnight,
walked with the old man
down to their bunkhouse.
The moon
was over it now.
The old man said nothing.
He cant talk at all
the woman had whispered
at the door, had an accident
in his throat.
So that was that.
They got to the cabin
& each had a cigarette.
He blew out the kerosene lamp
respecting their privacy.
He went to the bed
he had been in before.
The window faced west,
he hoped
he'd be asleep before
the moon came into it.

The old man was
winding up a clock.

He woke when it was dark,
the old man snorted
regular; even in sleep
his throat made no noise.
He got up & scratched
a wooden match on the underside
of the table, lit up the clock.
Three-thirty. Got dressed.
Outside the moon had set
so he walked from memory,
felt out the way. A barn,
a fence.
Two young bulls
in the bullyard. A calf
in a pen by itself.
A holstein near it, for
her milk. He opened
the gates, led the cow
& two bulls out, left
the bullcalf. They made
no noise at all
as if they had known him
all the while.
He led them
what he took for west
out onto the range.
He heard a scurry
behind him, it was the old
man, now dragging
on his sleeve,
stopping this theft.
He threw the old man
almost gently

to the ground,
stunned him,
though the eyes
seemed to be open.
Bright starlight,
no clouds.
He led the cattle
sometimes
not even holding
the halters
& they followed.
After a while
they came to the main
herd, moved through it
without comment
from the steers
& half-sleeping
heifers.
Once when he turned
he saw the sky
behind him getting
light. He came
to the highway
& led the beasts
over the cattletrap
onto concrete.
They followed
the highway
till the ground
west of them
began to rise.
He broke a fence
& led them
up onto higher
ground. A spring
just as it got

to be full daylight,
a little one,
enough for them.
He led them on
trying to think
what he was doing,
what
was being fulfilled
or what good it did
to whom. For whom.
Who was he doing
this for? The cow
mooed now,
dragging her milk.
Under a poplar
he milked her,
letting the milk
squirt onto the ground,
soaked in fast.
He made no effort to
drink. The bulls
stood around.
When the bag
was slack
he got them
moving again.
A copter
close overhead,
it would be
the rangers
checking him out.
He knew
what to expect.
Over the next rise
he led the cattle
down towards a thin

dirt track.
The pickup
came along fast —
There he is, Jerry!
he heard the wife
saying the obvious.
He & the cattle
were all there was
on that hillside.
The truck stopped
& the rancher
got out fast
with his rifle.
Juney & the woman
stayed inside.
The rancher
was saying something
he did not listen.
He got the bulls
& cow between him
& the rancher.
The rancher came on,
shouting.
He did not listen.
He balled his fist
& brought it down
hard on the neck
of the bigger bull.
The bull went down.
The rancher stopped
amazed. The bull
was unconscious.
He pulled out a knife
& opened it slowly,
crouched down & cut
into the bull's throat

& dragged the blade
down towards the chest.
He looked down just once
to see the blood was
flowing, soaking
into the ground
as fast as the milk.
Then he kept his eyes
fixed on the high sun
while his knife kept
working. He reached in
& pulled out
maybe the bull's heart,
something bloody,
spurting & dripping,
held it up
as if to the sun.
The rancher did nothing,
the man's spell on him,
his rifle fell.
The wife was crying
he's crazy he's crazy
& hiding her eyes
in her hands, but the girl
kept looking.
He moved quickly down
& grabbed the gun,
fired one shell
into the rear tire,
then broke the gun
over a rock.
With his hands & sleeves
& arms dripping still
with the blood, he grabbed
the halters of the
cow & younger bull

& led them down
in front of the truck,
across the track
& up the next slope.
In a little while
he remembered
he had left his knife
inside the bull.
Those people, the meal
last night.
He wished there were
some way
he could make them
happy. Or better
than they felt now
with their animals
taken away, tire
& gun wrecked, all of them
scared before breakfast.
It had to be
this way.
He hoped something nice
would happen to them
today. Maybe the sick
brother would get better.
It was a river
& he led the animals
down to it.
They drank
& he washed his hands.
Maybe on the bank
he'd find a boat.
Or a boat would come along.

# 12

Every story
as it goes
implies
every other,
as if a man or woman
could open in her behavior
a road to every deed.
And every narrative
would tell the whole story.
For a while,
caught in the beginnings of his fabric,
the old storyteller,
blarney-licking shanachie,
is happy. Everything
will fit in.
Just as a young man
if he's any good
believes that nothing
is impossible, & his life
will seize every moment
& do everything.
But each act
performed
is a limitation,
& the possibilities
begin to close down.
Not everything can happen.
The best of them,
Rabelais, Joyce,

the sages who wrote
Mahabharata,
the Odyssey, Lönnrot
between two worlds,
they tried to get
everything in.
I bless them for it.
Maybe the Dogon can do it,
who have reduced
every element of *happening*
to an ideograph,
& the thousands of signs
can be manipulated.
Or recognized
as natural forms
repeat them or mime them.
But *everything is possible*
is different from
*everything is done.*
An aspect divides.
The story
that seemed so promising
becomes only itself.
That is the history
of existential man;
it is not tragic
but it is less
than we could imagine.
The distance between
might be tragedy,
or we could make
tragedy out of it.
But mostly we make grief,
& grief
does not have the awe
of the tragic, the sacred

destiny
offered up in blood
on the altars of Mystery.
Grief does not have the wonder,
the *diesen Kuss der ganzen Welt!*
from which something
more than tragic
arises, & truer to our time.
It might be
an exaltation:
 at the end
 he became
 himself.
But there is a distance in me
senses that *himself*
as failure, even though by
common belief I would take
that as a man's best chance.
The distance is an edge:
a man must become
exactly other than himself.
To do the Other.
And break the story open again,
that the spiritual Seed
be not forever locked
in the material form: our oldest
prayer. Sun, take this
weight off my bones, these
bones off my Name
& let my Name
speak in the world
out loud alone.
Because the Spark
of *its* Nature
is free to participate
in every form,

yet the Form
of its Nature
is loathe to relinquish
that pinpoint of fire
& so is prone
to lock the spark
deep in the earth
of its formal substance.
The story ends,
under the hedge
the blind Teller
falters, ends
in a shudder
of particularity,
tracing in his mind
the wonder
he has failed, it
has failed, to include.
Inside the story
the Spark gleams,
groans, leaps
out in passages
of apparently
irrelevant description,
fastens on things,
weapons, colors,
a look recorded
in some eye, a silence.
The Spark, groaning,
understands
it must follow to the end.
And after that end
endure
another beginning.
A new story.
Some men have tried

to simplify,
solar myth, Freud's
clutch at mythologies,
Jung's archetypes,
Graves's beautiful
goddess to whom
every tree & every word
is of its substance
consecrate, to whom
all stories relate.
The notion
of a primal story
is wistful hunger
of the Spark
for a limit
to its wanderings.
But the history of the world
is the story of all its stories.
The Spark
is not delivered
until all possible
stories end.
And there is an austerity
somewhere in the mind
that wants to end them,
"hastening the end,"
to which every new story
is as sad as a new child,
begotten in concupiscence
(trishna), linked to death
& suffering, prone
to carry the chain on,
resolved not to be deprived
in its turn of any experience.
And so the existential hope:
a man

resolves to become himself
becomes himself
& ends his story.
But the story begins to swing again,
gets used to the spaces
in the mind it obsesses.
The shanachie hears it,
falls for it,
& begins to say.
The spark
maybe this time can move
the flesh *its* way.
The fabric
of the story
pulls tighter.
The old image:
a woman
at the loom
passing the male
shuttle
through the standing
warp —
the stand
of any story
is our shared
knowledge of the world.
Maybe a shared
world.
Consensus.
So the story
is never
for the teller
(the shaman
cannot heal
himself),
it weaves

through the stand
he shares with the world,
the spark
of his telling
enters
the hearer's mind
& instantly
a new story begins
that runs for a while
(the length of
telling)
almost parallel
with the first —
then
in silence
it veers
off its own way.
Efkharisto.
Eucharist & good day,
this spark
communicated.
What else is there
to give?
Ideas, opinions, pseudo-
records of pseudo-
personal experiences,
the fakes & flukes
of memory?
We communicate
a spark
& the rudiments
of a trade
to clothe it,
yarn
to make the weave.
And (sutra)

the thread
of meaning?
It is organic:
it is beyond
any intention.
These are the ways
of a story's happening,
its event
is the mind.
A meaning
is what is *found*.
And so the shadows
"close around"
the Hero-he is caught
in an adventure
he must follow
to the end.
The Arabs & the
writers to the Grail
knew a secret,
a way of weaving
story into story,
Sheherazade,
now takyth this tale
leave of Syr Gawain
and torneth
unto Sir Perceval
a while,
a while
to twist
& change,
keep all
the stories
going
& none
ever

allowed to end
except they fold
back in
to the ply of another.
At sunrise,
the legend is,
the teller dies
if he lets
the story down.
It is to keep it
going, up there
babbling
like a ball
played on the
spume of a fountain —
hollow
as like as not
but in that gap
or emptiness
allowing
a place for us.
The place to talk.
The Spark, concealed
but preserved —
preserved in concealment,
served
in concealment —
twitches & gives
off light
in the Hero's mind,
Herakles stifling
on the barren plain
dragging the shambling
stolen cattle
on to the end of his
world. And there

he sets pillars up
to mark
the place beyond which
no story tends.
I can feel his vast
sigh of relief
as the columns rose:
an end, an end to it,
end of the world
& no man goes beyond.
As he, the Hero,
cannot strive
beyond his story,
is locked there
the way the Greeks
saw their stories
locked in the sky,
unalterable narrative
of the fixed stars.
But they move
& have
their own motion —
little by little
the stories vague out,
move
away from the Pole.
And even the Polestar
wanders, in time
rejects
the fable of its north.
And Herakles,
no sooner was his
back turned
on his gorgeous
pillars all brass
& porphyry & gold

than some hooknosed
Phoenician
traveling salesmen
sneak through,
pragmatic as the tin
they'll fetch back
from Cornwall, the dyes
of Brazil gleaming
already on their sails
coursing indifferent
through the end of the
world.  It has
no end.  Herakles
goes home & finds
his ten labors
have changed to twelve,
he's off again
dragging a world
out of his memory
to meet it,
outside,
in the flat sunlight
of wherever it is.
A story
has only
a beginning —
maybe that much
is free to us,
in my choice
to begin or hold
a wise silence
& not yield
again & again
the fire
into the form.
*Give fire*

*to the fire*
the old text says —
& draws
a picture of it!
A man
walks down the street
he carries a torch
comes to a forge
from which the blacksmith
is unaccountably gone
but the fire blazes.
He brings his torch
in full daylight
blazing
to the fire.
The sun
is overhead.
A little boy
is watching him.

# 13

The river prospers.
The raft arrives.

*The point
having no parts, no mass,
is isolated
from every other part
by a finite distance
to which however
no minimum can be assigned;
likewise, in the universe,
no maximum.*

Solomon's Seal.

The scene of operations
is the Palace of the Djinn.
A singular
place,
      touted for its red
shiny marbles, little
puries the little
djinn thumb, beware
their eyes.

The Chief Djinn
is on his throne,
          a date palm
grows out of his head,

he unfurls his tongue
to lip
        the drop fruit.
Selah. He is Master
of the Legends of
Himself, no householder.
His wife is Mystery,
her pants
are always falling down,
nylon lined with mylar
lined with marble. They
with some accuracy
record
        the current
of her feelings. Litmus
lingerie. The world
between her thighs.
He knows. He puts it there,
as offering, every third
night through the year,
every night in Ramadhan.
He contents himself
with the taste of lust
left in her mouth
after she has proclaimed
her Desires. They shriek
away down the alabaster
hallways, snake
down the lazurite stairs.
He kisses her mouth
& tastes
her exploits. They
inflame him. He engorges,
possesses her.
Morning bash.
Then turns

to the Hall
of the Abysmal
Audiencia
where his attendant
peons have prepared
a travesty of justice
fresh every day.
Some shipwrecked merchants
are waiting his pleasure,
in the plausible hope
he'll send them home.
They are on some island
& have lit a fire
mostly of coconut husks;
one of them knows an in-
cantation he recites.
It opens an eye
in a nearby clam shell
through which they peer
into the Audiencia
& can be seen by the djinn.
One whispers
into the shell:
                    "Great Lord
of Djinn & Afrits!
Aloes on thine Unspeakable,
I caress
the levrorotatory
whorls of thine Ear!"

-Listen to this, says the
djinn boss to his wife.
-I despise
Phoenicians she says.
Get rid of them,
close that pismo eye.

Make it snappy — I have
a fantasy scheduled for
eleven, & after that
a session with the Teacher
of Brevity. He smiles at her,
she never fails him,
twenty thousand years
glacier or no glacier
she is reliable — never
once let him down unsatisfied,
or satisfied
more than he wanted to be.
She stomps back to her boudoir,
& he puts on his Cunning hat.

-O merchants (he cries,
though the shell has
good ears), O wanderers
upon the Unstable!
I have heard your plausible
supplications! What
can I do for you now?
"Send us hooome, o great
Lord of Djinn!"
                    -Where's that?
"Highag, o Lord, a little
port in Somaliland."
                    -Close
your mercantile eyes
& spin
on your left heels
thrice. Hig-Hig, was it?
"No, Hig-hag, my Lord,
the other
side of the straight."
-Start spinning, you're

home, drop in
any time.

        The clam
shut. The Lord of the Djinn
eyed his Vizier.
-Qlob, those sailors
dont come from Somalia.
Why do you suppose
they're so anxious
to get to Highag?
-I will look
in the book,
great Admiral.
The Vizier lugged out
*The Periplus of Everywhere*
& inspected the known
coastmarks of Africa.
-Highag, ah, it is there
that Seyyid Muktallah
ibn Juj of Isfahan
lies buried, & this property
possesses his tomb:
that those who visit it
thereafter are made conscious
of every act
in the middle of itself.
What does that mean, o Father
of Wisdom & Great Tree?
-It means that they are aware
of being aware of being aware —
some men are like that, & hurry
towards such intricate
awarenesses as we hasten
to the dewy thoughts of women
restless on their couches;

Qlob, shall I help them or
forbear?
         -O Great One, they
are there already —what is
help?
         -Well asked, o Qlob.
The Great Djinn turned
his eyes upward; when the wind
was right he could sometimes
catch a glimpse of the leaves
sprouting from the palm
above his head. He saw the leaves,
noted that they tossed
as in a smart breeze. Typhoon,
he said, make them a typhoon,
o Qlob. Or do I mean monsoon?
Something with storm in it
& much rain; sweep them
from the Afric shore
into the Red Sea again
where I can find them
in the bezel of my
lefthand middle finger ring —
I would watch
their consciousness
at work. Send down
onto their boat some rain,
& make the waves toss
a bale of hemp
or other most dangerous
herb aboard, no, let it be
the gaseous exhalation
of the Drug Qalab-qalab
confined in a bottle of brass —
just such an one as men
fancy contain djinn.

-O Great King, the copper
will be synergistic.
-I hope that's good.
-Lord of Dates & Mistakes,
it is as you would wish.

The Great Djinn
left the Audiencia
& went to his wife
where she lay
muffled in ermines
who swarmed upon her
& writhed between her thighs.
-One must have patience
for this game,
she sighed to him
as he approached,
& her flesh
trembled. Her eyes
are closed.

-Is this Brevity,
or are we still in
Fantasy?
              -No, no,
this is an exercise
my shaman-in-law
suggested, to make
the labia more sensitive
without wearing them out.
The Master of Brevity
has come & gone.

-Then send your pets away
& watch with me
a diversion, a maritime

enlightenment
soon to take place.
Here, in my ring.
He pointed to it
with a long abominable
djinn finger, nailed
in lacquered blue.
Each nail had stars on it
in the pattern
of the Ten Constellations
presiding over his birth
& other initiations.
(The Slipper. The Ripper.
The Reefer. The Two
Lepers. Simurg major &
Simurg minor. The Beaver's
Tail. The Artichoke.
The Sleeper. The Reaper.)
-Let me watch too,
his djinn-wife said,
my weasels have to
leave for lunch.
                    -Look here,
he said, & they got their faces
nuzzly close, her red
lips at almost the corner
of his eye, they were
wet with oil of musk.
First the stone
tuned in a war
with some GIs in sweaty
green clothes
carried a stretcher.
Idly the chief-djinn watched
the blood soak through the blanket,
rime with the color of the ring.

He flicked the dial
& in came The Storm at Sea.
They saw the three merchants
swept by waves
away from the seaside shrine.
Inexplicably, the djinn
began remembering
Gandhi's salt-march
to the sea.
That marched
a while
in his head
with what he saw.
His wife giggled
& he saw the three
tumble in the billows;
a log came along
(Qlob always was thorough)
& to it they attached
their self-possession.
He adjusted the volume.
"What a chance, we are beyond
the currents of our consciousness —
now our real minds
can begin to work."
The djinn heard that,
hmm, he said, that shrine
really works. -What shrine?
said his queen. -It's too long
a story — watch it for the
physical.
      Qlob now made
the log break in three
pieces; the merchants
cried out: "We will meet
again, we will help

each one of us get through.
Pay no heed to the ocean.
The force that
swamped us here
must exhaust itself.
Let us be carried.
We will reunite
knowing what we know —
it is only
a matter of time
& time's no matter,
but only
            that energy
by which
            we seem
to move
            from one
another
            now . . . "

The voices, ever fainter,
faded out. The ring
showed nothing but waves.
-That's a funny way
for drowning men to talk
said the queen. But the djinn
thought the whole show
was boring, flicked the dial.
The waves
were replaced
by a pedantic
Englishman holding a pencil.
"The point," he said,
"possesses no parts.
By this we must
understand

Boskovitch to mean
that in our modern sense
it has no mass.
Each point
(he's using the word
then in a purely
Euclidean sense)
is isolate
from every other.
The gap between
is not mensurable
in his system —
by the nature of the
cosmos his system
predicts (& his con-
cession to what Eddington
called "vulgar opinion"),
the gap between
is finite. Neither a
minimum nor a maximum
may be asserted."

The queen thought
commercials were getting
kookier all the time
but the Chief Djinn said -That's
not a commercial
that's religion.
They rose
from her couch.
She began to fondle him
& he, his attention thus
drawn to it, conceived
some lust for her, he
stole between her thighs
very smoothly, as if he'd

been there so many many
times before.

            I press
the Seal of Solomon
upon my eyes
to shut down a curtain
on their sordid
noontime amours,
they rustle like lizards
as they sway, half
erotic & half
ready for lunch.
My mind here disserves me:
it thinks about the Queen
of the Afreets, her scarlet
labia, her lure.
It ignores the instructive
Tale of the Three
Seafaring Merchants.
What I have learned
I've learned from desire
thwarted or got.
The instructions
do not make sense
until they link
with meat.
There is a purity in lust
I would learn
to communicate to my thought.
A man & a woman
interlocked:
seal of Solomon.
This image
has the power
to banish djinn

or compel them
to our work.
This image
has the power to
compel
"the enlarg'd &
numerous Senses"
to flower
in any being
sealed with this seal.
Eye
open in all worlds.

# 14

Rewards,
& banishments.
Whoever comes to this city
bearing the news
is first to suffer
the will of the city's gods
or the bitter will
of the olive & the goat
casting patience
like a shadow
on our burning eyes.
We are silenced
by the way things are.

By pain.
Most men
take it in silence
whimpering when they hurt.
And some make brave
jokes, persiflage
about the ineptness
of our condition.
Their brave
humor is worse than silence.
Rueful giggles
distort my ears
worse than the shrieks
of dying men.
It is not funny,

I will not
make the best of it.

Make the best
alone & absolute.

I will not be reasonable,
I have this famous
romantic trick
called *blaue*
*Blume*, impossible's
flower, sought for,
*The Grail*, savage
colored parrots in dark
trees, toucans,
herons on the lake, a tree
with articulate fruit,
quick fish, slow rock
of lamaseries,
freedom
to nations
imprisoned
by the sleep of reason.

Homage to Artaud
that he never
was content to be a man!

Lord of the bright world,
forgive me
my reluctance
to believe myself
when I propose
to be simple. I am not
simple, I am perplexed
day & night

by the anguish of Isaiah,
the incomprehensible
distortions of Ezekiel,
the things men do
to their flesh & wit
moved by what unerring
madness
to be not as others
tell them men are
in the world.
Masturbators,
mutilators, the wild
blackhaired young man
she dreamt of,
who jerked off
into a fire
inside the ovens
deep in earth, fire
whose only fuel & spark
to set it going that
gush of come
twisted, squeezed
out of his balls
both hands wrenching
to deliver —& that pleasure
he had learned
in a district of the moon
whose name
she could not remember,
but the delight he learned
had charred black
a patch of his heart,
grew larger or blacker
with each return
to the cavern ovens
where he burnt his substance,

exulting in each spurt.
Homage
to this shaman wisdom
that knows a man's
body is his tool
& tortures it
to make it climb
the seven-step treepole,
to make his knowledge climb
the ladder of the spine,
its Seven Altars of Agony.
A man who tortures women
is inaccurate;
he is trying to beat
the woman inside him
to make her declare,
make her crouch
on the birthing stool
& give him life.
Hurt her.
I beat the woman
to make me speak.
In the dream
he beats his meat
to make the fire
come & fire
fill the hollow earth
with a delight
so close to him
it scorches his heart.

This knowledge
is yucca & thorn,
oleander & what roses do
to those who love them hastily,
interpret

flesh
into a different
feeling, a knowing
hurt through itself,
experienced as pain
& known beyond.

Satan is the shaman
who failed his own pain,
turned away from the ladder
& spends his light
accusing those who move
into the pain & out again.

Not to be free of pain
but free inside pain —
"raising other men
into a perception of the infinite,"
& see by the light in their eyes?
Not hitting hard enough
to bare this nerve of grace,
ida, pingala,
& murder this sensory nerve
of the unsubtle face
that hounds me & my lazy mind
into a silence of distraction,
to satan, to veer from the pain.
Flower of dung
& rose-closed
cunt — murder
is in us, the blue
flower blossoms
at the end of ourselves,
tartarus, the acid soil
& laden vines,
alkahest, the pain dissolves

everything into itself.
Blue flower of not feeling.
Opium.
Flower of not being
anywhere. A Yawn.
That gap
is its chalice, the wine
fools the mind.
A word
        of nonsense.
Burn the wood
if it does.
The lute untunes.
Unstring me.
Hell song.
Let me loose.
The flow
breaks up
into its points.
No mass.
A distance between
I cannot master,
a different cycle
gears at me now,
torture inflicts
a change of Aspect,
leading to Diamond Body.
Nothing is perfected
but my notice of the fact.

[passé défini:] ". . . the preterite . . . is to reduce
reality to a point of time, and to abstract, from
the depth of a multiplicity of experiences, a
pure verbal act, freed from the existential roots
of knowledge, and directed towards a logical
link with other acts, other processes, a general

movement of the world . . . . Through the pre-
terite, the verb implicitly belongs with a causal
chain, it partakes of a set of related and orienta-
ted actions, it functions as the algebraic sign of
an intention. . . . It presupposes a world which
is constructed, elaborated, self-sufficient, reduced
to significant lines, and not one which has been
sent sprawling before us, for us to take or leave.
Behind the preterite there always lurks a demi-
urge, a God or a reciter."

It is here that music
resists the division
into times or tenses.
Is present. Unison
to which each man brings
his qualities, his "style."
Dividing (*scheiden*)
must be inside. The woman
pursued & subjected to pain.
Putting the devil in hell,
Boccaccio calls it. Rains
on the hill. All the ordeals
begin in her cunt, cave-oven
barred by grate, the interlocked
desires, too focused, too
goal-directed, make an iron
network. The fire must be puffed
hot enough to melt the bars
or he must bring to the oven
an instrument not connected
with his feelings.
Crowbar, brute lever,
much tempered steel & a little
cunning, pry it from the rock.
Every virgin was a harlot once

& knows how to aid
his analytic. The mortar
of the oven dome
is the weakest part, pry it
& bricks can be pulled out.
Leaving the original gap,
filled with the fire
he brings there
to warm himself with.

No, his hair wasnt black,
only the charred heart passage
turned black. His hair was brown,
he hadnt been to the moon,
only a friend of his, now lost
from record, came from that district
teaching this skin dance
in new places.
Modern glass doors to the cave
where the oven waits, cold now
since the dream is ended. Beside
the oven, a niche in the wall
with gentler heat, where bread dough
for instance could rise.
The mortar in old
New York buildings,
weak now, sifts out
almost at the touch.
Put up a century ago
with sand & long
human hairs, jet black,
oriental, mixed
in the mason's trough.
The water has dried out.
That's where the hair
is black. No water left.

*I can learn even from this.*

I am slow,
my hands are far away,
the music
closer than my skin.
Peripheral blurout.
Ordeal of earth.
These are ordeals —
to tear her veil
in the fury of his pain,
tear away the pain
that veils his heart,
burn heart, beat the heart,
beat the endless women of the heart.
The ordeals
are all day long.
Every night
is dream, every dream
an initiation —
to reach an irrevocable
*He Did*,
absolute deed
snatched out of context.
Silence of that,
our strife
is not with upper air
but the potentates
of our own despair,
our *complicity*
with the way things are.
We put up, & go down like flies.
Like grass. Like whatever
you choose,
till the rice is finally harvested
& we clear out of our houses

the dark furniture of pain
consequent upon the time,
implied by Balzac
& begotten
on middle-class proclivities
for sticking pins
in little girls. Bayros
in mind, his knives, the axe
the witch rides
with its blade
inside her,
inward razor,
ultimate reprisals
a man makes
against himself.
Congested city
of our conflicting wills
set so often
to deny or self-destruct.
Circumcision. The cut
off sacrifice, to start
life with a loss.
The woman carves
her lover's initials
in her skin.
   A tree
can surrogate, its flesh
bears the testimony
of what we wanted
to carve into ourselves
to make some knowledge stick.
I cut my arm once
slowly with her knife
to prove
   something,
what was it, I didnt gouge

deep enough, the memory hazes
& the scar is gone.
Why did I do this
to myself, what was on
my mind?
                    Sun Dance.
Self-initiates. The veil
of the body torn,
inner meat
the only Isis.
That the mind
be banished
from the streets
where it too easily
lingers,
                    the way things are,
the star of the likely
giving his comfortable
light. But Wormwood
is the star
where knowledge grows,
not serene, bitter, more
bitter than any sea.
Pain makes howl. This
speaks.
                    Mescalito,
turning the body inside out.
All the Sacred Emetics
of the desert, to empty
the body that it be filled with light.

There is no cunning
in our ways, we fall
for the old way. Hurt me.
Hurt me in her. Confuse
subject & object, reverse

the current of gemütlichkeit.
"Love what you hate,
hate what you love —
that's the way."
And this is our famous
technology of ecstasy,
read it
in every crime against the person,
read it in,
encapsulate the pain
& make it live
always inside.
Morbid fester. That's
where the Star Wormwood shines
on the bitter sea.
In its light
we see that the street
is not the street,
my hand is not my hand.
Tree not a tree.
Flower an emissary
from the Kingdom of Torture.
Bee sting. Spasms of childbirth
so that some new thing
can come out. Its turn.
Burn her arm, hold it
to the candleflame or lightbulb,
the years change
but this does not,
the opening eye
of agony
when what we suppose is real
shivers
to dream. I do not see the street
I see the pain.
It is raining & I love the rain

& I do not see the rain.
I see a newspaper:
sailor seized for burning
with a cigarette
his initials
on his girlfriend's rump.
What was she doing
while he did that?
What did she learn
while he, with her pain,
tried to experience
some hint of his identity,
to read his name there,
to make her him?
Old dimness of it, old
death, that a man
could find himself only there.
And another report, this time
less sure than a paper,
about a girl who
in sexual intensity
stuck pins in herself
deep, would walk around
all day long with the
pins in her, hidden
under her clothes, all the time
knowing herself in the pain,
carrying it like a chalice
of awareness, this thing
stuck in her no man could give,
something inside her, making
her herself. With every step
she knew
*it is not ordinary*
*where I am.*
We are silenced by the way things are.

180

Against the silence
pain clamors,
Artaud's cruelté, friction
of the alchemists,
hairshirt, Thebaid,
*stimulus amoris*, oxgoad of love,
to prod.

Pain teaches nothing but itself.
My hungry eye
is on the world & knows no patience,
& in the brittleness of hope
guesses there's another way.

Not pain, not the stoic
refusal to feel pain as pain,
not an equanimity
that becomes indifference
to your own flesh & others'.
Something else. I call it Work,
not knowing its real name.
I call it Work, it may be
another kind of torture,
this time not done on me or thee
but on the currents of Time,
as energy, bending it
to our use. Making.
Man is compromise
& I refuse the terms.
Animals are the teachers of pain.
Not be animal. Be
the other thing. The extreme.
The outside chance. Making
something somehow. Making
time to shape itself
around the wood or word or cloth.

Riding that. Be the other thing.
The afterbreath. The placenta.
The feeling that does not feel itself
but only other. The testicle.
(Homage to Artaud
who refused to be man!)
The staircase. The statue.
The object. Be the other
thing. The no name. The that
that is this. Not artful,
not a thing produced. Not a mask.
Be the other thing.
The ether. The new syntax.
The wall. The ridiculous.
The frenzied. The hidden.
The eater of food. The rider.
The goer. The thing
that makes experience. The man
in woman & the woman in man.
The conundrum. The trivial answer.
The lawless seed. The plan-less.
The map itself. The difference.
The wine glass. The magnet.
Be the other thing.
The broken sword. The dead tree.
The snow. The listless pond
covered with fallen leaves.
The wheatfield. The springtime.
The artery. The doorknob.
The grammar-book. The flame.
The outcome. The space
inside a house. The bird
on the roof. The underfoot.
The miracle. The inaccurate.
The crack in the wineglass.
The charred paper. The ruins

of an old church. The chimney.
The cow. The distance between
the tips of her horns. Her horns.
The mountainside now in sun now
in shadow. The interval.
The zero. The blind man's mirror.
The coin. The empty bus.
The desert. The saguaro. The palm.
Be the other thing.
The ink. The hairbrush. The needle
of acupuncture. The alkaloid.
The beachcomber. The friend
who does not stay to supper.
The star. The crayon. The this.
The compass. The man who just left.
The hose. The smell of something.
The what I forgot.
The other thing. The process.
The god.

# 15

How different you are
wants to be said.
Baring your flesh
to a nest of mirrors.
All the glass
are the eyes of me.
Fortunate to see you.
And what they see
see nowhere else,
a difference
from every one
in deed & motive.
You are content
to be silent mostly,
confident
that no discussion
would say you plainer
than you walk.
The way you do
redeems me from
the way things are.

# 16

I want to change my mind.

Guesswork.
The more the
heavier again.
A walk
down some rock,
with beasts
for company
flit
by the corners
of my eyes —
not looking for them,
the panther
puts me in mind
only of women,
the lion of me
coming towards her
lordly & hungry
for love, timid
only of the species
difference. Coyote
the other night
bottom of the drive.
Looked up,
too far away
for me to see her eyes.
Gauguin's
fawncolored girlfriends,

a businessman
to the end.
My foxes.
I'm the old
Goatbeard, I caress ye
with the immaturity
of my immortality,
I rode here from India
sodden with your glances
but my penis slack —
a marvel
when you come to think of it.
I thought,
& that was the end of me.
Who speaks?
Three times I dozed,
the glasses
fell from my nose,
V-2 rockets landing on London,
we must get away
into the country
where your dress
will cover my mind, your blue,
svelte hips, what was her name,
nodding over my eyes.
I made my way home, New Years lawn,
zero somewhere in Queens,
high el station, the bakery
nearby closed.
Candied almonds,
suck-stones —
slurp the pastel tones,
innocent
impressionist.
                    Turquoise
for Christmas. A button missing

from my vest first time I wore.
O sew it to me. Advance
into the asthmatic air, the cold
bronchioles. A bowl.
Dustbasin. Pelvis. Come lively
smell of garlic. An aromatic mind
smouldering from the pine-torch-drip
resin from other peoples' weddings,
gold afternoon, the chupah, doves
released now inside the veins of my hands,
nerves. A tree, without wind.

Piano, old style, postMozart
but not much. Snow today
on Angeles Crest Highway. Linda,
was her name? Raving, I smashed
her cup & she was quiet, understood.
Got it all wrong, she thought
she understood, I let the cup
of her hips slide, I did not catch,
the whole valley, faltering
in the magnetic drink. Drink this.
Feel better? I want to feel
more than anyone ever felt.
Saw. Tasted. Took
time to change the music.
She put bread
below the cheese, made sense
that way. She was not naked.
She served herself & her friends
on some broad leaves
culled from my mind's stream
before sunrise. Crisp curl
of my cress. Salad
of Imaginary Girls here
come into flesh, too far

across the room for me to reach.
The only thing worse
than an Imagined Woman
is an Unimagined one.
The olive, the wine,
any meal
that is not sacrament
destroys us to eat.
Affinities.
If I sit down
to "break bread"
with any but
the circle of my loves, then
I have blasphemed against
my life & work.
This food
is eaten
to nourish a long song,
a song & dance, a bush
for lots of men to beat around,
to find a way, an away, a work
that sustains. Then only then,
famous olives & rich
sauces with a backlight of wine.
Clarity! I cried, clarity!
but now my bones fear
that shine
is made to serve some end
beyond a man's hope
to coax a song again
out of his mattress or celebrate
the newest rising of a sun.

"clarity is a purely rhetorical attribute, not a
quality of language in general possible at all
times and in all places, but only the ideal appen-

dage to a certain kind of discourse, that which
is given over to a permanent intention to per-
suade. . .Political authority, spiritual dogmatism,
and unity in the language of classicism are there-
fore various aspects of the same historical move-
ment."

I will nail these
enigmas up
to help us all
from powers.
Tufts of soft grasses
rich from new rain
but dry enough
to rest your head.
Comes out by itself.
I will not give you
heaven & hell —
I propose a texture
so dense, intricate,
snaky with thread of gold
& honest old scythian wool,
that it will take your eye
& hold it better
the closer you look.
While I, in my Arcane Apart,
keep the structure up my sleeve.
Soft sleeves of arnel
stroking which
(just before dawn, you
sleeping, the whole
fucking world asleep)
I fancy myself to touch
the body of woman.
To be sure, it's my left
arm, & surer, you made me

this shirt. Which is as close
to Tiresias as I come —
any other body
of interest
only when the woman
is gone
(& always the woman —
I call it so, to keep
my interest, & for
to be accurate —
woman inside, my soul,
mi alma
tantrically chingando
mi corazón)
(her many arms & legs
wrapped round tight,
disguised as
coronary vessels —
I'm no stronger
than she is,
but with luck, as strong).
I hate a place
where I'm alone with men,
whether they're friends or not.
A night spent with men
is a dinner with no meat.
For that She is
(& Lady thou art)
my nourishment.
I'm talking soul-eat,
not oral games.
Riderless cycle
through the wheat,
the lovers rest
on hills of chaff,
their nearest neighbors

voles in runs—
as long as they have each other
society is in good hands. A day
when everybody fell in love
& then the sun came out.
That's how it must have begun
on Third from Sun, our own
big E, our motherless Tlas.
Who fell in love
with the image of mothering
her children. The wheat field
is kindly today, a little cold
but the sun bright.
Returning to the mood
of something before mothers.
Not the moon.
Trying to be clear?
To be near!
                    Texture
is not decoration, it is
a more intimate structure
yearning for your close
attention, tension between
you & what you see
more fertile than any valley.
Change my mind in the window.
Change my mind in the ground,
*Grund; Ungrund* as destination,
at last to be where No one stands?

The Lady Isabella held my hand
when I was nervous of the sea.
The two boatmen were incomprehensible,
much as they talked & sang.
I sang with them. Isabella, Isabella,
I came with you

to change my mind.
You & your sister (Isabella: "I have
no sister")
                    & your daughter
("I have no children.")
must surround me
in this apple boat
("he's off on mythology,
let him rest, poor man")
& take me
inside your bottle,
chain me a millennium
& let me loose
when the Kingdom of the Spirit
is at last alive among men.

Isabella held a flask
up to my lips, bitterness
of wormwood & anise sweet,
I didnt think
you could get that anymore,
must be twenty years
since I tasted that
(the Marques de So asked,
"What is he saying? Is he
haggling?" "No," she said,
"he's just been out too long
at night.")

        Isabella, when I was four
they took me to the World's Fair.
What I remember is incredible
brightness in the French pavilion,
brighter than daylight. My father
talked about the Iron Horse, Isabella,
is it like that now?

"Hush. (Is that
what you say in America?)
Hush. We have not yet
even come to land."
Must it be an island,
Isabella? "*Must* it?
What a strange question.
It is an island, & we're
going there."

           Isabella,
I want to change my mind.
Is that an island where
the mind is changed?

"Listen to what the boatmen
are singing,
           *A lus a tenerb*
*pietamos el alro,*
*na la alra noi pateuns*
*tras el moar azerb,*
do you understand?
By light & dark
we seek an Other
but the Other (feminine)
waits for us
across the bitter sea."
Is it the mother, Isabella?
"It is my mother."
I dont want it to be mine,
ever, I want the motherless,
I only came with you
to change my mind.

           "Maybe
we can help you, maybe not.

You were calm & courtly on the ship —
why have you blown your cool now?
Are you just afraid of the water?"
Lull said it was machine, I dont
want to be part of his machine,
but to use it, use it. Where are we?
"An hour from land. I'm beginning to regret
we took you with us.
The book we'll make from you
will have the discipline of order.
Imagination is more demanding
of discipline than any science is;
undisciplined science makes
only for inefficiency. Undisciplined
imagination destroys all proximate life."
Proximate? "Your own, & your friends
& lovers go down too."
But I made an Essay on Form,
I listen to the heart —

     "but do you hearken,
that is, obey? A heard heart
is just background music, soupy,
unless you obey."

      Homage to
Beethoven! I cried.

     "It's not
as simple as that."
Opus 110, in A flat, I said.
"Deep yearning
for male friendship
(those tenor-baritone
duets in Verdi!)
for which you expect
to get a woman's credit,
a woman's thanks. It will
never happen. No woman

is interested in
the form of something else."

Isabella! I cried, I thought
it was different where we sailed,
so confident on the white ship
dawdling west. "But now
we move west quickly. Hear
the throb of the engines."
I heard nothing,
                        just the wind
& the lapping of the sea.
On an impulse
I reached over & scooped
a handful of water up & slewed it
in her lap. The sea is just
itself, I said. "Who said it wasnt?
Now my dress is wet—does that
make you love me better?"
Want you more. "Perverse."
Turn you over my knee & spank.
"Quick! what part
of your mind is that?"
Bend over.
Over my right ear.
"We call that
the Hole of Intention.
                        Where
do you feel it when I question?"
It's a little resentment, down,
down under my left ear, almost
eustachian, almost in my throat.
"You can surely see from that
how far resentment is from center.
Even anger, usually, even at its
reddest, holds the edge only

of the mind. Now I'll bend
over your knee if you want."
No, the time is past. It was an
infant pleasure, throttled in the cradle.
"When he was an infant, Hercules
strangled a python in his crib.
From which we must learn
that only strong desires
have a right to live."
Did I really want to beat you?
"How could I know that? I'd guess
you were trying to upset me,
distract me from some location."
Right ear. I told you. Right
ear. What I really wanted
was to fondle you.
                "An ugly word.
You mean be infantile again,
that's not interesting to me, I'm not
involved with psychology, only
with the brain & the mind. I have no
interest in motivation."
(Isabella! Isa bella!)
"At most
            in conversation."

Isabella, the soft
of your buttock, your right
buttock, Isabella, I imagine it
innocent, teenage tender, Isabella,
I need to feel you in this boat,
this nowhere, it's so dark, I know
you're soft there & unknowing,
the tenderness, the tenderness!
Isabella! Your face before you were born!
Isabella! The faces at Hiroshima,

the knowledge that corrupted them,
I saw them, the horror, they are so
hard, the keloids are like rock now,
no grace, charred, they have seen
what no one was supposed to see,
the crack of knowledge, the crack
between matter & energy, it blinded them,
Isabella, it melted their eyes,
Isabella, only in your flesh, the soft,
only in the trivial can I be saved,
save me. You were alive then, you knew,
you understand, just now you said it,
there is no sense in motive, there are
no motives, only flesh & what it feels,
the flesh we pay no heed to, the unseen,
uncared for, Isabella, I turn to that
in the extremity of my despair,
there is no good in searching or knowing,
everything that is known
burns off some skin, burns its way
into the scarred mind, the book you
make of a brain is a book of torture,
records of where the knife went in, Isabella,
only the soft skin will save me,
inside your thigh, under your arm,
below your shoulderblade, places
you have not worn away, Isabella,
tabula rasa, Isabella, no records kept,
nothing but the air alive & my body
moving to you . . .

                    "Your problem
is you do not
believe in Nature.
By Nature I mean
the way each percept

responds to the
energy of Time.
Static you want it,
infantile, bland heaps
of blond flesh,
undifferentiated.
The Protoplasm Kid.
You come close
to disgusting me –
but I still offer
our hospitality
on the island
in return for your
geographies."
I'll do anything you want.
I told you
I wanted to change my mind.
I want to believe in time,
after long years to come
to believe in your face,
not just your skin.
"But why are you saying
these things to me? What am I
to you?"
            No idea.
Dont need ideas. Dont trust ideas.
You're a woman, & nearby.
What else rules
the Harmonia Mundi
but that proximity?

"Change your mind!"
On her word I plunged
my hand in water again,
Ego te baptizo
in nomine Patri ignoti

et Fili incandescentis
et Spiritus Sancti radicis
mentis, Stimulatoris
perignoti.
　　　　　She slapped me,
saying she had no need
of my religion, & that all
those genitives were awkward.
What do you expect at sea?
I asked, calmer now, almost
at ease. It is blasphemy to travel
or sit down to table
with those who do not work
in my religion, I said.
"Cant you wait till we get
to the lab & start the book?"
—she sounded tired, had been
keeping up a good fight,
hadnt napped as I had.
"Why do you suppose
everything you say
is interesting to me?
It isnt, you bore me,
you bore me terribly,
always the same
sort of stuff, breaking
into lyricism & smug
when you do, exalted,
phony, irish."
　　　　　Isabella,
you are some kind of chance
for me. I dont know what I
am for you. "O wait till the island,
wait till we're home
& can get everything down.
It's your geography I want.

All the rest
is personality, style —
what we need
is location.
Change your mind!"

I leapt over the side,
paddled along beside the boat,
one hand on the gunwales.
I will take my brain
& its old palimpsest of locations
& find a world, I saw it once,
beneath the sea. Or beneath me.
Softer than your skin. Newer.
I resent your boredom,
I abstract myself
from your narrative.
She said nothing, offered
me a hand as if to help
me back in.
        No, I shouted,
you are going
only to the island of propagation,
far out at sea
I hear the shudder
of the generative mills,
I will not go
& be an islander again.
I was born once on an island,
& once is enough.
"But wherever you go," she said,
softly but I could hear, "you'll take
that book with you, that brain.
You will write it & it
will write you. You will never
be sure, never be clear."

Clarity is the least
of my problems.  I swam out
maybe twenty feet, treaded water,
o Isabella, one thing I ask,
throw me a garment of protection,
a Leucothoe's veil
to help me still the sea. Women
have that power.
Throw me your panties
& they will carry me
& I will carry them
into the intricate city
& work your salvation
along with my own.
"O what does all that
*mean*? I cant stand it,
I'm glad you jumped,
go away, go away!"
But your panties, throw them
to me! The Marques de So
withdrew himself
from contemplation at the prow
& called back to her,
"You heard the man. You got
each other into this. Give him
what he wants. Dont haggle."
"But why does he want them?"
Because they held
your only innocence,
now throw them to me!
She wriggled out of them,
tossed them halfway
between me & the boat. I dived
& came up close, grabbed them
& turned away from the boat,
swam hard. White nylon,

they swam with me, in my right
hand (interchange of tinctures:
the right hand of a man
is electric), between strokes
they floated, like sea-foam.
There wasnt much to them
but they lasted till landfall.
I waded ashore on the beach
at Venice. It was getting light.
I wasnt tired
from what may have been my swim.
Or a swim. Anyhow,
I was on sand. I buried her panties
below tideline, scooping the wet
sand out a foot or two deep,
covering them over. God is good.
The sun was rising
on the other side of the city,
a good hot California sun.
I walked up the boulevard,
figured if I walked
the sun would dry my clothes.
Six or seven miles, a couple of
hours. Where La Cienega crosses,
I sheltered from the glare
under a freeway overpass.
There was something
I had to remember. Mallorca.
Ibiza. White clothes. A journey
interrupted. I hated something,
what? I hated narrative,
hated the past tense
that plagued my life,
sucked attention away
from the tender skin of now.
That's not all. Something

chained me to the street,
I hated that. How far
can a man walk in a city
without becoming an outlaw?
Where was my car? Away north,
in the San Gabriel Mountains,
cant even see them in the smog.
Clothes dry, wrinkled.
Walking & by bus, by mid
afternoon I was at the zoo.
Felt an odd reluctance
to go in. These animals, they
know something that we dont,
but it does them no good.
They are condemned to a present
we hunger to reach.
They are trapped
& we are trapped
by what trapping them
implies. An order
we can impose. A discovery
I did not want to make.
And yet the fact of travel
forced me. I had been there,
had come here. What
line was I following? Where?
I couldnt stand there all day.
There was an order & I knew it
perfectly well, for all my finesse
& trickiness. It was there,
had its way no matter what
I did. A city. I was beginning
to be sorry for what I'd done.
Or not done. Or getting into a story.
Or getting out of it.
A life

exhaustion of possibilities,
systematic
as my energies can contrive.
When there's nothing left
there's something left.
The trick of it.
A girl with cotton candy.
For instance. Stickum on her chin,
for instance. Dry eucalyptus leaves
she lets the gluey cone fall on
when she's done. The years
she will experience. Her tongue
cleaning her chin. Two boys with her,
each pretending not to notice her
as much as they notice her.
The mother with her cubs, her eyes
no less trapped than I imagine
the inside animals to be.
Gobs of selfpity. Glop
of when I have not looked enough
or gone
to where it is. Why not go in?
Why are there so few mirrors
in public places? Yucca, mi amigo.
Hey you look tired,
why dont you go home?

My soul, her many legs & arms
wrapped around my heart, pumping,
interchanging ecstasy, in & out,
heart cock, sun cock, for a little while
hold all the rhythms together.
Not to describe. Go through.
Only the strongest desires
have a right to live.
Ophiuchus overhead, a dragon

no man throttles. The Bear
turned away from the Pole. Dark
early. No stars yet. It must be
feeding time, I hear the lions
roaring with carnal intelligence,
about to know
the truth of their time.
And Truth is day by day?
What is this mirror I wander in?

I hitch a ride in a Volksbus
all the way to Pasadena.
Friendly guy, a longhair,
he has his group, the music
they share with him
becomes his life. He trusts it.
I tell him, awkwardly,
I cant trust
anything I dont make.
He laughs & points to the dash
where a little picture of Meher Baba
is scotchtaped over the radio.
Next to it is another, interests me more,
his girl, wearing something shapeless,
a nice smile & a lot of hair, vague,
on somebody's back porch.
I watch her. One of those dry
purple flowers of succulents
is tucked behind the snapshot,
if I touch it it will fall apart.
I want to ask what year this is,
Baba seems four or five years too late,
the girl is faded, the bus is old.
I wonder about his music.
It keeps us quiet. I want to know her name.
If I ask he'll worry somehow,

dont want to worry him. I'm tired
of asking questions, especially
that sort. You're too close
to the brink already, I'm not
going to push you any closer.
Respect a man's distance
from the abyss. Homage to Pascal!
There are vortices also
of the finite, great swirling gulfs
where the dimensions clash & multiply
*inside* the object, whirlwind of relations
between any object & its ground.
*Grund*. The girl's face,
indistinct, a warm kind of smile
perhaps worn for the occasion, learned
from a folksong, from an ad,
whatever we still have left to teach,
learn, break our balls to master,
maybe a way of walking, pelvis swung,
left hip, right hip, a smile
from the machine.
                    My friend,
I want to know your girl's name.
Instead I ask him
what kind of flower that is,
Cactus, he says, some kind of cactus.
He drops me at Del Mar & El Molino
before he turns south, to his girl's
he tells me. Still no name.
The junior high school kids
have all gone home. Streets easy.
I walk up to Colorado & across,
get the bus up Lake. After a while
it occurs to me I'm home, puff
the last short hill from the
end of the line, come up the drive.

There was no reason
for where I'd been.
It opened nothing.
But maybe what it closed
can help me, "save" me
as I said to Isabella.
I'd better forget her
as soon as I can, for both
our goods.
                        But lust
is the only thing I trust.
(Why didnt I say that
to the kid who drove me?)
And things have changed.
Mr Acosta
has cut out
the oleanders.
The roses out back
need watering. Later.
The black
mexican raingod
squats in the dust. Eet ees
not as simple as that, señor,
no hhow. You cant come hhome
so easy as thees. No.
And the table says,
Because you avoided
typographical errors
do you suppose
you can come home?
Home? Hemo? Mohe?
Meoh? Meow. Not even the cat
can permute
to your advantage.
Dont try to hang it
on the cat — you like your

reality that way
sometimes, but what of the night?
Declensions of nouns:
things are in relation.
Conjugation of verbs:
deeds matter how you look at them.
Finished? Finished by nature?
Not finished yet? Never?
What a homecoming.
A few books on the shelf,
enough for a life.
The radio: Mainland
China admitted to UN.
Picasso's birthday.
Where had I been
that men grew no older?
The banana leaf looked up & said:
somewhere you cant tell me.
No better answer
from the honeysuckle
trailing down the roof:
You have gone somewhere
you cannot 'communicate' —
try a song or dance of it,
to give the feel.
You cant have it all
or tell it all. Do
what you can.
But I will not make
the best of it.
Where nothing fails
but the words I mutter,
I will be silent,
sullenly, not at peace
with my incompetence.
Dark now, almost.

The hibiscus trumpets
are closed down, against
a morning when they sing
the same thing again.
Bless them, there is sense
in that. Say it all
over again,
but say it all.
Write everything.
In ten thousand years
we have only scratched
the surface.
In another ten,
the surface itself
will be worn away.
Will we get to
the fruit we posit
beneath the rind?
Sudden death, slow death,
everything that
distracts me from your skin
& you from my attention.
While there's some light left
I ought to walk around,
& back there,
growing out of the dense
stand of bamboo, a tree
too ordinary looking
for me to notice up to now
suddenly has big
green lemons on it, hard
to the touch, will ripen
while we're still around.
Our own lemon tree.
And rose hips
on the long

trailer of the rosebush
that bends across the path,
a danger in darkness.
I refused
any conversation
with the lemons
but went into the house
feeling better
for their being there,
come home & find
a new tree.
I had solved nothing.
At least the journey
(the sense of going)
was real. Was.
The sense of narrative
chokes me,
always another
story to be told.
The trip. One feeds
into another, dawn
never comes to deliver
the teller from his tale.
Or the cat turns
almost to greet me,
her tail her balance,
some work there
for me to do,
work of the scales.
Outside I can see
the stars whose names
I never learned
have filled the sky.
Helen asleep,
I go to wake her,
my mind filled

not with where I have been
or where it's been in me,
but with the lemon tree.
Helen, waken.
And while she's coming
from the room I can never
enter though I sit at her side,
the lemons ripen
in my mind,
thousands of them,
more than our tree
will ever bear,
lemons alive, sharpest
yellow, blended with nothing,
filling my head with their light
layer on layer,
white out, bright out.
*This color*
*is more specific*
*than you can say,*
I hear in my ears,
a woman's voice, Isabella's
in reproach, Helen's
in encouragement?
Or a bright schoolgirl
with blue cactus flower,
filled with all foreknowledge
of what she will become
(wife & mother & part
of the machine), & in the free
light of her little time
absolutely mantic, saying
the wildest things
because she doesnt have to
live up to them. Knows she wont.
Puts it on me. I have to live

that specificity.
Helen, let me wake you
with lemons, not yellow ones,
hard green, no good to us yet
but they are our own, I mean grow
where we grow, from the same
ground. Helen, I have talked
to so many women, heard
some few answer,
I called out to them
to say it to me,
they spoke, took some burden
from me & gave me some,
absolute past tense, it did & I
went with it
& come to you now
with rumors of lemons
let me wake you with.
Share this tree.
In time,
the fruit of it.

# 17

Woof of chance
arrange
me through you,
my will
is through the light
of your eyes,
incline to me
smiling
half-nervous,
the care you take.
I can say it all.
Lake
in which I knew
a drowning,
all metaphor
vomited
when I looked at
you through
whom I am now
proposing to go,
with you,
travel
with & inside,
dog my mind
to the furrow
in you
where it changes
where it must
change,

dreamy
hillside
a goddess
standing there
revealed in sea-colors
& looking down,
distance
of your eyes.
Mary, Mary
you have come
upon the earth
to bear again
a man with a reason.
It grows with me
it sticks to me.
And though I fall
in love
with a woman
betrothed
to the sun,
though I cast my shadow
on her intention,
she receives me
in your name.
I call you
because the blue
of your robe
instructs me,
you must be a woman
underneath, I call
to that beauty,
Mother of God,
open your robe
to me
because you *must*
be beautiful,

I know it
from the sparkle
on your sea,
I can feel the rocking
of your hips
as you advance,
roses in your lap
draw me to one rose,
thrust of pelvis
as you step on the moon,
you master it,
bring life there,
flora & fauna
of insane vacancy
come to terms with life.
Your heel.
The snake
you ride.
Ten red flowers
that are your own.
Nine mysteries,
thirty years
just to open my
eyes & know
mystery is there,
eight angels
to caress
the cleanness
of your skin,
I must come to you
as I am, a man
or nothing,
accepting the compulsion,
loving the lust
that moves me to you,
which is the blood

of the only world we share,
Mary, seven swords
I must lift in turn,
wield
against the secular
in my mind, pierce
the familiar trappings
in which they have
hidden you from me,
woman, that the lust
inside you
is so terrific
all the powers of God
hurried to fill you,
you danced
all your life long,
you never
were sated, not even
death quieted —
you fell asleep
in lust, lust
to be yourself
in the whole sky,
lust to be more
than knowledge
or opinion,
your roses
insisting on miracle,
you taught there is nowhere
love cannot transform
if it does not go flabby,
six gates of your body
filled with delight,
Virgin. Virgin:
intact delight
never yielded

to the machine.
From your intensity
a man was born
who would not be man,
needing no father
but the lust
you knew the world with,
Mary, that you hear,
that the spirit
or whatever we mean
when we cry that
filled you,
& you kept it alive,
nourished it graceful.
Did not keep house,
did not allow
time to fox you
or your child.
The world is your robe
& you wear it
intensely, splashed
with all its waters,
burned by every fire,
the muddy, the confused,
you wear our anguish also
as a garment
over your naked body
whose curves & hollows
fill out the robe
again with meaning.
You live so strong
you cannot die —
I pray to that strength,
that I can come
past your robe
& the pious nonsense

they've hidden you under,
let me come to your thighs,
dark nipples
that swell when any mouth
comes to your breast,
intact delight,
harlot of Nazareth,
unwed mother,
enigma of fire
burning all records,
impossible accuracy,
full lips
like yours
were never general,
you swallowed
the Meaning of the world
& let it loose again,
laughing, speaking your heat
in the shape of a man
anointed by your womb,
who would come through
& in his own turn
dance
& die to teach us dancing
but the words, most of them,
are lost. What I have
is you,
at last, after all these years
to know you as a *woman*.
Womb. Oven of our sense.
Tower from which I can see
again & again the daylight
fill the fields with color
& the night permit
every embrace. Mary,
because you are so filled

with grace, heat of being,
transformer
of all energies,
teach me to transform.
You sit on the ivory chair
of your own flesh, your lap
is secret & full of light,
jewels fall from your hands
because you are woman —
let me come inside you,
vase of chosen seed,
you pick who comes in you.
Like any honest man
I would come to know you
& would come to you to know
my own powers
at your extreme.
Because you shape
all energy
your son works wood
with the hands
you conceived for him,
works matter,
hangs on matter & dies
not altogether out of it,
his dance around the cross
where you stood
sorry only
that not all men & women
would dance with him.
Arms of the cross
& he dances,
with Mary & Mary & John,
the loved & lovers who knew
his gospel was an energy
made new in matter,

sent therein
also to dance.
The dance is too serious for grief,
love too quick for laughter,
so your grief & his smiles
are not recorded,
the texts are lost,
men make them up
reasoning from family relations,
from the blood craziness of Greeks
& the sense of hearth
as economic unit, you laugh
at them, you pour
filth on the clean floor,
let clothes
fall where they may,
never
wake anybody
up for work
        you break
away from all that, all you
Marys, Miriams, it is not
ordinary where you are.
Mary go free.
Mother of God
you are least of all
a mother,
        *theotokos:*
who fleshed a god,
give birth to something strange
in a man
because you are beautiful
& the men of Languedoc
taught me you open your robe
to show a dark body
happy to receive, yield

its delight to the world.
God me.
   The fierce of love
knows itself in you.
You have been hidden so long.
Only the gypsies remembered,
came to your caves
between mountain & sea,
Carmel, Marseilles, places
where the human body began
to know delight & know itself
in the same instant. Black virgin
of here & there, Pale virgin
of Freyr's cart, beechland, palm-
land. Come to me
as you came to Lucius
over the sea
& let your name
be only the beginning.
Let me pass through you
& change my mind.

# 18

Wood
of change
to range
me through,
my will
is till
& never
from,
my form
may discipline
the song
of changes,
age
of silicon
age of carbon
hardening
in the dens
of my successive
wills.
Inorganic tree:
who would
forgive me
if I climb
& time
be wrong?
Remoteness,
long
agreements
with purpose

turned
to renew.
Now
at last
to visit you
to secure
your purity
to lure
my form
to this
engagement.
Elements
scattered,
the wizards
long ago
lost ac-
curate count.
How many?
(A voice
in fog,
soft, alto,
subdued
beneath the
bitter
arches,
asking of me
How many?)
I can know
only
what pierces me.
How many?
Feet
& hands
& eyes &
broken nose,
ears

& fingertips
& slipped
over the
whole
world my
skin,
rock mantle,
sphere
of hidden grass
& public flower,
my sex
concealed
by bushes,
the maidens
rush
up from the sea
not understanding
ocean
is no tomb
& no tomb
is solid,
not even
this hour
holds.
(She asks
again,
the elks
of Caledon
vanish
into fens,
the towers
raise
only in me,
she asks
again, How
many?

my answer
would crack
us both
wide open,
O lady
dont you know,
cant you
feel
even in this
dark
the limit
imposed
by the nature
of the thing?
No sense
to ask
How many?)
This balance
is a balk,
a ladder
firm
but nowhere
at the top,
of all
evasions
none worse
than this way to
vanish in air,
a cross
purpose,
a memory
boiled
out of an old
confusion,
pure,
limits of the

world,
not what I reach
but reaches
me.
I rise
to remember,
we both
can know
anything
only
when we two
are pierced
in each other,
stuck,
turned
inside out
then I look out
from your
eyes
& what I see
was never me
before,
wet meadow
a broken arch,
the aqueduct
gushing still
its gravity
fall
to waste
the water
where it can
never
be used,
this mineral.
What can I do?
(She asks,

How many?)
what can I
do if suddenly
there is no one
out there
& no one looking
but the air?
I thought
it would be
One
when I had
subjected
my erect
city
to your vast
geography
or built me
there
where you were
most various —
with reason
I thought something
would come of that.
Naked,
gladly,
I climbed
& naked
you were climbed —
your form
knew mine
& the numerous
I thought
singled
us there
where we
mutually

rose.
*Others*
*you saved -*
*now save*
*yourselves*
they cried,
but she
naked
as I knew her
& with her
friends
naked
at her side
whispered up,
*How many?*
*How many*
*are the elements,*
*we never asked,*
*too shy for that,*
*& now up high*
*you've forgotten.*
They were
weeping
but I had not
forgotten.
You & I
bled
into each
other,
the numbers
were perishing
under us,
it was hard
& hard to
speak.
I watched

their nakedness,
was moved
to love them
clearly.
What I had
I used to
speak,
I told them
Three
must be Four
when the woman
comes to mind
& Four
must be Five
a little,
just
this broken
hour
& for such
as me,
I'm Five
enough
for all of you
& when I pass
the Three
go into
Four
& the Four
be One
& the One
remember me.
After that
it will be quiet
& the One
will dance
with what

I can not explain —
it will not
be Two & not
be None
but One
will not dance
alone.
Then I let
my head hang
down
& watched the
numbers
crumble
& the ground
crack open
& I heard
their bare feet
slap on the rock
like the feet
of people
dancing
& I knew
that whatever
you & I
had discovered
in each other
they also
in some
kind of sense
knew too.
We rested there
a little bit
lifted up
above the hill
until the both
of us

were only carbon
& even that
much of form
defined a song,
one
that others
have leave to
sing
since you & I
are done.

# 19

To say it all.

Everything,
in twig or fruit or flower,
whatever stage
of its juvenescence,
perfect or not.
Or the only perfect
thing is something that
is.
    Moving through the known world
to what I dont,
        to hear
what voices
        speak in me then.
Legitimate
exploitations of the sexual
parts of the tree,
        gluey splendor
meant to attract —
only to disperse those lovers
later, soiled with
a sense of itself.
Everywhere.

Aleph flower.

O I'll give you alphabet
& comedy, a pleasaunce

where the measure
of the sarabande
is not lacking, evening,
fickle torches
reading the wind's mind
& dancers all of them
timid
            from the start of the world.

There's nothing
a dancer wont do for you —
surround her with pine
& system,
                    transformations
nestled in night.
                    By day
it's all milkweed & awn & glume,
bee paths & ant intelligence, blues
& browns, attempts
to violate the secrecy of flowers.
But at night the dancers begin
& their timidity
is old as the world, the bodies
for a little while are only their own,
suddenly
            they're not afraid of me
& the beauty
            of their intimate postures,
small-talk they save for their friends
tender little sexual jokes
pour over me, I become a Liber
of their forest, forest
of their movements, their legs
trap me, I love them,
they make me crazy, sane,
I am the woodman

of their holy groves,
                    the manyness of them,
            their names
are what they do,
perceiving them
                I lose at last
all sense of myself, I am lust, lust alone
to know them any
way they can be known.

That's a sunrise kind of dance,
& all people
                within my sense of them
are dancers,
                or mind that Gideon place
where they begin to move
over the autumn casts
of a deciduous human culture,
books, facts, melodies & friends.
Snakeskin, & they renew.

Because I want to watch the dancers
I know there's a phœnix in the woods,
old, aching
for Arabia,
                wanting to go down into itself
& rise

        A judgment
        in the ashes
        of the burnt
        hillside,
time to renew. Reliable dancers,
educated loins!

                In these last sweet days

before the book is closed
        & something else
opens  beyond conjecture,
I turn away
from forms of knowing
any society
imposes,
            I want to know all ways,
them all ways,
                & suddenly Things
are my allies again,
why not the door & the key,
why not the tree & the razor & the pear,
why not the tread-worn tire & the egg,
miracle of the frying pan, why not
blue bowl of sky
with eggs smashed in it, why not
the book & the feather, the stone
& the sneaker, mason jar, bobsled,
a pair of jeans, a troika, a sonnet,
why not whipped cream, quarterinch drill,
house, hod, cod, ling, basin, footstool
of the Most High?
                Every object
            is a microscope
(telescope)
            through which I perfect
my always knowledge of you.

Method:  By moving it
        in relation,

                    by comparing.
By contrasting. By putting
it in you or you in it. By
writing it down. Erasing it.

Rubbing it out.  By touching it lightly
against where you were last.
By timing you with it.  By holding you close
while it ticks or barks or smokes outside.
By loving you while it does what it does.
By doing what it does & pretending
that I'm loving you.  By doing
what it does & loving you.  By loving it
& wiping tears from my eyes,
by remembering you, by doing
"what would please you if you knew."
By pouring it over you
& eating it from your skin.  By eating you
& remembering it.  By being
all alone by myself in a large space
& holding you both in mind.

# 20

Every error
becomes the text.
Oak gall. Mistletoe. Those stones
the chinese used to collect
that looked like
something else, no matter what,
& stones that cut & polished
revealed some happening inside,
the grain became (say)
two friends saying goodbye to a plum tree
while a heron
walked away over the lake.
Mirror of minds, Rorschach
& other mistakes. Not mistakes.

The pool of ink
my slave must peer in
to apprehend the lovers
where they flee from me —
I hunger for both of them,
her beauty, his horniness
I also want to possess. The ink
reads their likeliness,
the way their romance
carries them. Now at sea,
now eating noodles in a southern
port, they lie in his hand
& so in mine. Read the ink.
I do not read in my own hand.

So the lovers run
& tracing them
I have no need
to reach out & re-capture —
the penetrations of their need
lie open to me
in the boy's naive eyes, his shock
sometimes at what he sees,
the fearful way he watches me
watching him. Network of mirrors,
& those I pursue
imagine themselves free.
The land itself
interprets them
& every passing bird
(or one that sits
just preening
upon their conjugal bush)
is an agent
of my diligent
scrutiny, diligere,
because I love them
& it's my love
wont leave them alone.
Confessions of Sulphur,
with a true account
of my marriage
& our son Cinnabar.
The children
pour out, successive,
yielding a salty taste.
What I see
marries me.

I close the book
where it opened before,

having gazed at the page
learnedly for ten years.
Close it, close it,
the wind moves
in the palms, the City
long foretold
turns its
green lights on
& sapphire
lap
its pools,
a human city,
where the only
birds
are the white
thighs of women.
From the top of the world
the angels of Enoch
pounce down on them,
fall
to our ground
in love
with the daughters of men,
instruct them
in all the typographies
& all mistakes
flow from the languor
of their caresses
after the sky seed
was sent in,
full
of its own
unmistakable meaning —
text
itself
breathed in

someplace between
the sun & my right ear.
I strike a match
& peer around the cellar,
lo! sesame & love's
ingenious oils,
all the mistakes
are part of the text!
Every color corn
has its destination,
no mistake
to find a blue kernel
at the 156$^{th}$ position
counting from cock-crow.
A work of my timid age,
when my delight
still ran to numbers
& to the kind of sweetness
numbers best relieve.

With hosannas of unrecollection
& the morning stars
all together shouting,
the cortex confutes itself,
blanks out, I am left
at the end of October
gasping towards life
in the only world I know.
I sit five minutes
outside in the sun,
a million years old,
a lion, something,
face to the sun,
glasses off, shyly
my arms open, warmed
all the way down,

sun zap in hypothalamus
or wherever pleasure is,
its center, chakra, house
in our city,
    touched it,
carried me
out of the cold wind, out
of any time. Brought back
by the thought
to share it with you
I came inside,
    the sun set,
it is ridiculous,
domestic comedy
which is also
our commedia
leading to
the silence
at line-end
where the song
begins,
    commedia
rising
as at Easter
to the articulate
silence
whereof the definition
is nowhere
& the Sense is everywhere.

The song.
Towards it.
*Great Pause*
Bruckner marks,
who knows
how long it

lasts?
      one sabbath?
one sæculum?
And now the sabbath
is begun,
the candle lit
& the godwoman
enters,
shadow-cloaked,
starry-eyed,
compound
of many conditions
we anticipate
by life on earth.
She sits
by the wine
& is no less
the wine
as it pours out.
The table set.
My wife
serves silence
on a pure white plate,
we eat
in lust,
the woman
who is sabbath
is entirely
inside her now,
I am alone with her,
I am almost
alone with myself.
The drug
of sabbath
works very deep.
Sabbath poppy,

sabbath
synthesis,
chemicals
of self-possession
deepen
like the guttering candle's
flicker in the still
full glass of wine,
the color
called ruby,
hard as the sun
but something's harder,
it looms behind her,
we can taste it clearly
only on the empty spoon,
the glass of water
I insist on,
        I will not drink
      the sabbath wine
        except from the lips
       of the sabbath
& that's no wine,
           but our water,
the hollow spoon
so lovely empty,
light on silver,
light on steel,
reflection
as if of water.
But pity him
who thinks this the sea
when he holds
it all the while
in his hand.

A glass of water

on the sabbath
with you
I love.
You bring it,
I am free
to drink,
clear glass raised
about an hour to dawn,
this mineral,
this stone.

# 21

Jive
I said.
Taking
on *jiva* & Slavic
*zhiv*-,
   life, to be alive,
to live the life
proper to your nature.
Psyche's need
is how to be alive.
Psyche's question
reduces to (that dark
questioner, that
woman)
   How do I know
I'm alive?
O lady. O epistemological jive.
Vivre sa vie
& all those Parisian
elucubrations,
built out around & concealing
the moist center
of any thought,
con/cept,
   the apprehensive
(prehensile)
   loins,
whence our any
take on

like the world.
More jive,
& getting dangerous
day by day
to dodge the issue
of living speech
*la masse parlante*
of all who take these
ways with us,
talking, talking.
Not an opera.
A mass
of mispronunciations,
deviations
from a grammatic norm
imposed by Devils
Elsewise Unemployed —
every mistake
(I swear it)
is the meaning
of the text.
Hermetic,
Hortus conclusus,
the sealed garden
or garden —Hortus Claudius—
of the lame God
who is the Master Mason
of all Europe,
labyrinth-wielder,
architect
of all the gardens
closed to me
by distance
& my sessile ways
prone & supine, erectus,
prone to respond

at length,
          gravely,
but not go there.
O woman
to whom only
I have ever travelled,
& then even
not enough
to prove
I meant it,
I mean it
beyond anything
I can say.
All the rest
is journalism,
the fashionable shill
of cities
distant (ewig)
& all the blue haze
I fall for
time & again,
which are not
places we can talk.

But every error
is the meaning
of the text.
The places I love best
are the ones that turn me
more newly towards you —
& there's no
orthodox in that,
only geography.
Only the mode of life
to live it
proper to each being,

to find that
& record it day by day
in the fact of it,
living.
How lovely
to be so obvious,
*beso*, the mistake
brings back
to the fact of us again,
the mistake
is the meaning of the text,
obvious,
the obvious garden
of the hidden God.

I leapt the fence,
awkward, pulled
a muscle in my thigh,
charleyhorse,
                    limped
around, got to what I took
to be the center,
found an ornamental
water there,
lotuses in it,
closed for evening
though the sky
was bright enough still,
an orange
incandescence in the west.
Found a pavilion,
in it nothing
but a polished table
empty, & some chairs.
I sat & watched the grain
of wood, this tabletop

cut from one tree,
the rings growing
year by year more regular
away from the tortured center
which began to hurt my eyes.
The grain, was it,
or was it a map of
diseased cells
instructing my body
through my eyes,
a picture
death to look on?
But the world
was my bride,
this fear
did not become me,
I worshipped the wood
a while,
but still
the whorls of that center
& the vast space
inside the smallest ring
so much bigger
than any other
gap between, that space
was torture, why?
Ginnungagap, a shadow
of dark meat inside,
a terror, why?
as if the first act
of anything
is anguish
& all the rest
a convalescence
from that primal thing —
birth trauma

of which our lives
are echoes,
our consciousness
only the story
told over & over of?
Bullshit, I cried,
the table
is only itself,
the wood
is good,
the tree
remembered itself
& left these spaces
for me to remember . . .
mine?
   I got out of the tent
as fast as I could hobble,
met a man
coming towards me,
a girl walking
a little bit behind.
They stopped & watched me.
He turned to her & said,
See, that is the Lame God
& we are in his Garden.
I wanted to deny it
& make them understand.
But I had nothing
to be understood
& instead of denying what he said,
asked them how they'd gotten in.
The question
seemed to confuse,
they looked at each other,
she said  I came with him
& stroked his arm.

I reached out & touched her,
between her breasts,
she stepped back & a change
came over her. The man
walked away. What is it?
I asked her, What have I done?
I'm pregnant now, she said,
our mutual love
is forced to fruitfulness.
She trailed away after him,
sometimes looking back at me.
I stood stupid a while,
then followed them. It was
getting dark now, it took
a long time to catch up
where they rested in a clearing,
the man holding her shoulders
while she sprawled on the ground
fondling a baby.
She held it up for me to see,
big balls for a newborn child,
but his eyes were closed. It is
my fault, I muttered, I can see that
now. The man said nothing, seemed
not even to notice me. The new
mother paid all her attention
to the child. I walked back alone
& presently came to the pavilion,
lighted now, & someone had set out
a good dinner on the table.
I sat down & ate. There was no
bed, so I went outside
& lay down to sleep beside the lotuses.
They were open when I woke,
the sun was high. I had hardly
gotten to my feet when a naked

boy, fifteen maybe, came running
fast at me from the forest.
He was the newborn of the night —
my knowledge of his fact
gave me strength to
cope with him now.
He tackled me
but I did not go down.
I threw him, crashed
across his body & worked
some damage on his knee.
Then I let him up.
He rose, tried to walk,
fell again, got up,
limped towards me.
My leg had healed
overnight, I left him
quickly, said only
I have business
with your mother.
I searched for her
throughout the garden,
found the corpse
of his father
but no sign of her.
What is her sign,
or any of her signs?
I thought, & thought
I spotted some
among the trees,
movements of bluish
slaty birds,
finches later, last
of all crows,
but each of them
when I followed

led me back
to the middle pool
where the boy still
stood, looking at the
lotus pond, crying,
looking around, drying
his eyes, smiling,
crying, looking.
But I went on
to search every
sign of her
till there was no sign
& I came at last
to the fence
at the end of the garden.
This time
I got over it
without injury.
In the dusty path
I thought led
back to the city
I saw footprints
I took to be hers,
having nothing else
to follow
or to trust.

# 22

A secular waking
& I want to find
the holy *in* that.
Mushroom or mountain.
The hills of La Cañada
tilt away from sun.
"An ordinary morning."

"Because to exist is to exist *in time*. But the
ideogram conveys more than this. It projects the
notion that this energy is to be conceived of as
*over and against* temporal successiveness. That
which is without limit is locked in confrontation
with that which diminishes and destroys. In time,
all things pass away. The timeless is *at war with
time*. Since ALEPH is beyond limitation, this war
is endless."

Somebody hammering
next door,
                    very deep
throb, a drum-like
confrontation — rubber
mallet & fender?

"The upper component is a *hammer*, signifying
this non-actual, invisible energy of ableness-to-be
ascribed to ALEPH. The lower component is a
*leg*, standing for that which walks in steps: the
succession of temporal duration."

The hammering stops
long enough
for me to think of Egypt.
Aleph hidden in Beth,
a house.
       In Egypt,
*B* is a leg,
complete, from foot
to knee.
Halfway home.
Next door
it's tapping now,
very gentle,
as if the secret
were close at hand,
gate of open-sesame
on the verge
of swinging out.
Batter. Futuere.
Foutre. To strike
repeatedly
          demanding
entrance.
       To knock on the door.
To fuck:
       in Israel,
a mistake
still common
with new speakers.
It is not a mistake,
it is the
point of the text.
Yod. The insistence
to get in.
       Comes down
in little tongues.

A nice
metal,
        clatter,
hubcap
hits the driveway,
unmistakeable.
I want to go to La Cañada
where a drug store's
having a sale
of colored markers,
cassettes, jampots,
the Old Straight Track
to the heart of matter,
Angeles Crest Highway
(Route 2) bending
up the mountainback
that we look out & see
what we walk around on
in successive
legs of time. Stepwise
progression. Scala.
Silence. Sometimes
I expect applause,
shower of gold
hitting the chessboard
(was that Morphy?),
slithering down
in Danae's lap, my
girlfriend, my viennese,
my demi-blonde.
My Klimt. From whose
rosy lap I would eat slurping
Schlag' mit Erdbeern,
mushy, all mussed up.
No, morning.
Elements of Style.

New World trees
& other vasculars
needed to heal.
Cinchona? Teosinte,
Theobromus. Yerba
mate, a leetle
on the insipid side.
Glass of beer,
blonde, Schwecater,
Pschorr; Spatenbräu?
Darker. North of Alps
men live in a long
pink dream of women.
This is not
without its effect
upon Kultur.
The Ghost
of Raspberry Syrup
stalking Europe,
stylistics,
formica,
          the Great
Entsiklopediya
lined up on the shelves
pointing north to the mountains.
Floundering
in a dream of style.
Pale, primitive
color process,
a famous painting,
homestead
in Siberia —
east of the Urals
the color changes,
it is the ruddy
tawny dream-cap

of amanita,
Tarnhelm itself
of the Varangians,
& no more pink.
The gush
is yellow,
like the loess-rain
on Central Asia,
bile
of Prometheus
our patron
stretched out,
sphincters of Oddi
torn by beak,
digest no fat.
Only the creamy
inwards of mushroom —
which is firm!
is a pillar
& its dome
a little lifted up
above the forest
mulch, cast
of birchbark
(runar) & needles
of the needletree,
pinus.
      Hagia Sophia.
I close
the encyclopedia.
No one
in the library,
the intimate
librarian
has gone home,
her glass enclosure

locked. From
up on the eighth
a view
over the whole city
or I can turn away & hide
in the comfortable
alcove
among *Chemical*
*Abstracts,*
so many years
of detail
also stretched out.
I find
what I'm looking for,
not the womanless
peace of books
but a vault
of information
tended
by the maidens of
Love, who are
mistresses also
of all Lore;
they are fierce
& beautiful,
Elektras
guarding their
father's grave,
old Saturn
his fertility
& the golden
autumn of his reign
when all intelligence
tended
to *them*
under the birches.

God, I want to look at
birch trees
this afternoon!
I'm a week away
from the library,
the journal articles
safely xeroxed,
not yet read,
held
against
"An Ordinary
Evening in"
Paradise.
When the now
sallow golden
leaves of the
birches
cover themselves
with writing
& runes
grow on the pale
bark,
        natural,
daughters of Lore
& intimate women
not far
from the secret
of books,
            those
pneuma-
transmissions
also
given to me,
stored
in the dance
of those women

declaring
more by the lift
of their arms
lowering
a book from the shelf
than the pages
thereof are likely
to remember,
a pure information,
how she bends
to lift up
the atlas
she bought me
for Christmas
with two hands,
world in mine,
the use of it.

I close the memory
because the sun moves
& the way the leaves look
now against the garage wall
means I'm not as early
as I thought, the time
has been forehanded,
moves, bright sunlight
beginning to pale now
as it does before it
reddens, Goethe
looks across a field,
prism in hand. Prism & pen,
the only
artifices
he allowed his perception,
to see them,
to get them down,

the "deeds of light"
filling the world
with intimate knowledge.
Of itself, & what it
mirrors, aleph-light
previous
to any perceptual
system, even a star's.
*Narrative*
*runs quickly*
*but when it's done*
*the sun is gone.*
And it's afternoon,
& I havent seen birches,
havent gotten the car out
& traveled
up into the mountains.
Why did I let
those wants
be muted? Why didnt I
do what I wanted?
Because a want knows me
& I am in its hands?
The day heals itself.
No hammering.
Ter quaterque. Empty air.
Extraordinarily clear,
empty. What moves?
What of those flames
I speak of
pouring from our flesh?
The life
proper to each house,
foretold by the structure of.
The life, the livingness,
is elsewhere.

Out to lunch.
I pass an etching
in the bathroom, Dutch,
a very strange tree
like a crouching devil
with his flaming mouth
gesturing
towards an empty, strangely
undetailed landscape
with his arm
& his arm
is a naked girl
leaping
from her crouch
out into the same
empty air.
A windmill,
to remind,
too sketchy
to grind corn.
Lost
in celebrating
daylight
I look up
& it's dark.
Complete.
As if I had watched her too long
leap into emptiness,
only the Form of her body
meaning anything to me
or being
          the only definition
of that place (that time)
(this time)
          I would accept.
Not *too* long.

There is an oven
in these matters.
Growth anticipates form.
My hands
allowed for
space between,
folded now,
enclosing
what has been given.
A miser of it,
unwilling to restrict.

"The SHAITAN who hinders always 'settles for
less.' It cannot refuse to let the game be played
. . . but it tries to curtail the scope of fulfilment
. . . trying to fit into the framework of ordinary
existing life . . . where one tries to keep out of
trouble."

And suddenly the lust
(even the lust for more)
becomes a service
of the Queen.
                    Break
the devil Put the devil in hell.
Sulphur. Where he longeth.

The ordinary day
becomes Kabbalah,
is put to bed
where it rises,
in splendor
                    (in dungheap
contrive the pearl),
in orient
an erection

to compensate
for what goes down.
The colors of it,
carefully graded.
The oven
rests.
        What I found
was what wanted to be found —
no rape intended
on those Daughters of Lore
who continue
a veiled tradition —
the man who takes his time
comes at last to Isis,
up the steps
one at a time,
                heaven & earth
baffled by his slowness.
He winds up the jade clock,
puts out the ruby cat.
The weathercock
always points east
(a secret
in his left wing) —
maybe tomorrow
the wind will
will what I want.
Thermostat
set to wake.

Isis
is a day.

Her veil the brightness
on everything
& my response to it.

The small words
coaxed to speak.
Prepositions, particles
of which my name is formed,
pressures
from which I grow.
What house is this?
The least I could know.
Aleph.
      The imbecile
who wears my clothes
pauses
at the summit of the stairs.
No good the sundial now.
Dont bother looking
at the red carpet
from Bukhara, the truth
of the matter is not there,
left behind
when the sun melted
over the dwarf poplars.
Isis is a day, come to her
along the corridor
of seven turns
past the twelve niches
all of which
(such is the winding
of the hallway)
point to Mecca,
all of which
remind you of a stone
fallen from the sky
called Heaven
onto the stone called Earth
& no man heard it fall.
The arches you enter

are put there
to divide
& to remind.
Autolysis. At some moment
it will be necessary
to go into dissolution.
Cadaverine. Enzymes
of leaving the house.

But now the story
is of legs, shapely ones
in nylons, shapelier
in whores' fishnet,
old dumpy legs cased
in black cotton, old
women of Sicily
widowed into black
who crawl up the aisle
every morning mass
on their knees, looking
for heaven, husband. Isis,
her child not yet found,
the women
moving
around the throneroom,
come to her,
they all
are dancers,
choked on knuckles,
dead fingers, smooth
hands, mistresses,
wives, the Dancers
surround her,
come to her,
bring her her child.
The imbecile

gathers his forces,
his tongue out
to suck what he can
off the wind or whatever,
he trembles
to get air in his muscles,
he farts, he bats
his longlashed eyes,
holds his balls
through his pocket,
he staggers forward,
his left hand
hides his face.
Wings
sprout from his shoulders,
he becomes
an Idiot,
advances,
he is all by himself
where the hall
grows wide,
dont look at the carpet,
the weaving
has magic in it
that would fox your feet,
keep moving,
Idiot Alone,
cut off from the merry
dogs of society,
the book
falls out of his
hip pocket,
lies behind him
like a turd,
memory
of an impossible

dinner
fades in his mind,
suns rise & set
through the meaningfully spaced
windows along the hall,
dont count them,
there is nothing there to count,
keep moving.
But now he stumbles
& scatters
a flock of partridges
camping on marble,
old women in black
help him to his feet
roughly, they've seen
too many,
the young women
fart in his face,
the smell reminds him
of rain on a city street
in summer, after a long
dry spell, the likeness
almost catches him,
he begins to turn,
the young women take pity,
turn him again, tell him
to forget. His feet
do it. He achieves
a forwardness. Bees
fall out of his hair
& take their prearranged
flight formation
before him, riddles
of the fixed stars,
constellations, he asks
himself about his Sign,

almost remembers, moves,
blessedly he forgets
to remember, the sixth
turning is near, why is he
so dark, cant he say anything
to all these women
leading him on?
What women?
What am I talking about now?
On? He hears men
hammering on goathide,
brass kettles, he refuses
to hear them, the hall
silences.
             A window
ahead of him.
The sun rises
one more time.
*This is your last distraction.*
He turns the corner
& becomes the door.
That is nonsense,
he says to himself.
Now he's not an idiot anymore.
He can dissolve.
One by one
he disjoins
the panels of his heart,
four cast out,
pulls out the nails
& separates
the frame,
two cast out,
solves himself
inward
towards her,

he's in
her room now,
all her attendants
have fled
or been dismissed.
He approaches
her where she sits
in urgent beauty upon
a throne he cannot see.
You are yourself the veil!
he cries to her,
his first words.
She doesnt change.
He might not have spoken.
What he'd said
sounds stupid to him now,
what he remembers
of it. She
says nothing to him.
He's left his heart
to enter the room.
When he remembers that,
he knows he has only
one thing to say.
He says it to her,
quietly. I
am what you mean.

# 23

Watering the tenderness
that hooks on. A train
into a speculative country.
A twelve-chambered heart
to teach succession in time.
Some kind of mistake
has been made. Sollte dieser Mann
verunglückt sein? The train
dark by the siding. Two lamps
flash alternately red. No sound.
Five miles down the river
a bird sits in the signal box.

This is the last crossing
before the border, except for one
little used, up in the swamp,
where the right-of-way is much
higher than the land it crosses.
The bird does not want me
to go away. The sign
confuses me. It would be better
if I were braver. Half an hour
waiting for the train to come,
when it would take my car ten
seconds to cross the tracks.
I dont. No sound of a train.
Eventually the bird flies off,
the lights go out. I cross,
& move up the hill, past the

strange house where marriages
disintegrate, past the churchyard,
go north at the intersection,
in three miles strike the dirt road
down off left, towards the river
again & that last crossing.
I can leave the car there
pulled up beside the track
under the tall grass.
I go on foot along the tracks
where the only danger
will be the low trestles
on either side of the island,
less than a mile each, & then
mainland right up to the border.
The ties are easy walking. No
train for hours. But I hurry
on the trestles, dont relish the thought
of dangling in the marsh
with an unscheduled freight
grinding overhead. This is not
meant to be adventure. It is a
crossing. Nothing in my mind.
The best way.
                    Hier ist das Moos
zart! Mozart named from, here
the moss is soft. Some nonsense
fluttering in mind. What might
lie behind it. What demonic
lichenologist
                    whispers in my head.
No one. Not even a fear
of the trains, of not
getting across. I'll get
across—the problem comes
afterward. How to *be* there.

In a few minutes, nobody
around to watch or interfere,
I had crossed the border
into the matriarchy. Bushes
were more of a menace
than the borderguards — why
didnt they watch this easy
way in? Maybe they shared
my disquiet, that the problem
is not getting in but sustaining
some kind of life inside.
Bullshit. No snakes. An owl
over at my left, near the river
neutral to all politics
which still kept on beside me.
I stuck to the tracks; the first
station was closed for the night —
the customs entry a few miles
further along. Halfway between
here & there I left the line.
It was close to morning
& I didnt speak the language.
I went to sleep beside a log.
I was in; now everything else
was up to them, whoever they were.
When I woke up the sun was plumb
over my head, a man on each side of it
looking down at me
like incompetent scientists.
Nal strómun hen amáryak?
one asked the other, & the other
said Bíldresu, bíldresu, nal piel
karánami.
            I said, I admire
the absence of fences. What
is over all of us is the Sun.

Otherwise we have nothing in common.
I got up, they let me, one even
gave me a hand. Zar, he said,
niul pénemi ent sagrónnin.
I dont speak your language,
but I'll try to sense. Where
are you going to take me.
Or are you going to leave me here?
Their maroon cloaks were stitched
a little down their tunic sleeves,
so one opened his arms
not unlike a bird. He
put the cape over my shoulder,
& gave me a shove. That way.
Do you admire Sibelius? Na grat
ech mi, na salát nimm brára —
it sounded brusque, they moved me
along. I didnt know what to say.
Or strictly, I could say everything,
with utter freedom. But unconditioned,
the urgency of speech diminishes.
It was unimportant. I went
in silence. They hustled me
into an old Buick painted
the same color as their capes.
One on each side of me, front seat.
The car went slowly on an empty road.
From the lay of the mountains
it was clear we moved north —
at least they werent dumping me
right back over the border.
Which is the worst that could happen,
right? Just to make conversation,
I said, I cant imagine how come
I've lived so close to the border
all these years & never picked up

your language. They said nothing.
After a while, the driver
began to sing, rather well, baritone,
something Puccini-like. The other
officer said Skar, the driver smiled
& sang louder. What could it mean?
The road went along between low pines,
with bigger stuff, deciduous,
back a few hundred yards from the
road. Nothing else to look at.
As long as he kept singing
I didnt have to talk. I lit a cigarette
without offering them any.
I smoked. It tasted stale, a lot of dust
had gotten into it, perfumey,
I hate a sweet smoke. Two schoolgirls
walking along the road,
long blue dresses, they smile
at us as we pass. The officers
smile. I do not smile,
just to keep the relationship
clear. I am some sort of prisoner,
I'll be damned if I smile at their
women if they dont treat me right.
What are their intentions? Skar,
I say tentatively, the driver
smiles at me & sings softer.
No zlu-it pek amóryam? asked the
other. The other. Bugger off,
I said. He smiled. Why are there no
houses? Then I said it aloud.
No answer. Not even a shack,
no light poles, no phone lines,
no signs. I like your unspoiled
condition. The driver said Mórmor.
Mórmor? I questioned. Mórmor mic

albamósi, trúde, énnat?
                              I guess so.
I was tired of it all. It meant
so little & I had expected—
maybe not much, but something,
something. Not these birdmen
& their jargon—come to think of it,
they lived near the border too,
& apparently couldnt speak mine.
The fault we shared. You're also wrong
I said to them. Do you know what I mean?
No answer. Ahead of us
down in a hollow,
some sort of town, stone buildings,
a flag looking strange on a steeple
instead of a cross. What town is that?
I pointed to it. Skar, the driver said.
Maybe it meant yes, & he was answering
what he thought was my question:
are we going there. Try Skar for yes.
Skar, I said. We stopped in a kind
of little square. Not a soul in sight.
They led me across to the middle,
a hole about ten feet deep, maybe
twenty feet square. They shoved me into it
suddenly, so I dropped all wrong,
turned my leg under me & hurt it,
bad. I lay there, startled, resentful.
Nothing to say. Leg not broken
I think. Hobble on it. Get up. No
purchase on the wall, to climb. Dirt
floor, crumbly dirt sides. Maybe
I could carve steps in, take
a long time. The side would crumble
before I got anywhere. Wait.
Hobble around the walls for exercise.

Exercise. Nothing to do.
                              By nightfall
one corner of the hole had become
my privy, dumped there, peed.
I scraped dirt up to cover. Then
the rain came down just before dark
& went on most of the night. Strange
how we flee from rain. Relax.
Get rained on, it made
a kind of comfort on my sleep,
though I woke aching all over,
sniffling. My cigarettes
were soaked through. The matches
ditto. That day was warmer
& by noontime I'd gotten set again,
revived, my muscles relaxing
in the overhead sun, glanced
off the pale dirt walls, made snug.
I walked around a lot, to make sure
that leg didnt go stiff. All day
not one person looked down.
Hungry. Nothing to eat. By next
morning the hunger had settled down,
didnt bother me much. It had rained
again in the night & this time
I had sense to drink it as it fell,
& scooped out some hollows, spent
a lot of time doing it, hollows
with little channels running to them,
they filled up while it rained
& I drank a lot. But ten minutes
after the rain had stopped
the water had all sunk away. Well,
I'd had enough to sustain life,
amply. By the fourth day I began
to worry deeply. The sun went over,

the rain came down every day.
The hunger was talking inside me
& the stuff in my head
was no comfort. Less said
about that the better.
But on the fourth night
I had a dream-guardian
stand over me in sleep,
he taught me a song to sing
& showed me how to clear my horns
of their moss in the right season.
When I woke, I couldnt find
the horns but remembered the process,
repeated it in mind all day,
along with the song. The horns
had to be rubbed on a shaggy tree
when the Agate Moon was half full.
Not half empty. They'd gleam then
& feel much better. Close to dusk
I happened to forget the song,
so that night he taught me again,
I think the same song. Maybe not.
It used up the fifth day, when no
rain fell. And none on the sixth.
But I didnt forget the song this time,
& called to the rain, & sang to it,
wondering if it could hear me
from the hole I was in. I spent
a lot of time sleeping, the rest
walking along the walls, enlarging
my earthworks & reservoirs,
in case the rain. When the rain
did come, it landed hard
& kept at it. Soon
I was up to my knees in mud
& fine water. I drank a lot.

Hadnt thought of eating the mud,
it felt good going down
but then woke up
my stomach again. Stomach
began to cry.
The song
sometimes helped & sometimes
made it worse. When I was careful
not to let the mud go down
my belly stopped being hungry again.
That was good, & I had plenty
of water now. Even hours after
the rain stopped, I still stood
in the slosh of it. I drank & drank,
always careful to filter the mud
& ball it up against my palate
then spit it out. Drink more.
Started raining again; got an idea.
I began to claw at the wall,
it slimed away under me, but after
a long time a pile of it had fallen,
I was burrowing vaguely upwards,
as if continuing a groove
only slightly off the vertical,
but enough to crawl up a little.
I began to work hard,
& counted on the dirt above me
to come sliding down. I could get
over it, push it under me,
stand on it, pack it down,
I was getting somewhere, tunneling
upwards, even the cave-ins
helped, gave me more footing
down below. I did this all night,
& that was good, I kept my eyes
closed, kept the dirt out.

I had the sense I was moving
upward. By dawn I had reached
the surface, actual ground.
All I had to do was roll over
on my back, one push of my arm,
& the rising sun looked at me,
no walls on any side.

                  The square
was empty. I drank some water
from a horse-trough, wandered
around town. All the doors locked.
No one answered. Why were there
no women? Any woman
would have helped me now.
But I wouldnt forget the song.
I wondered if I was meant
to go south to my home or try
moving further north. I wondered
after that what *meant* meant,
& how a man could be said
to be meant to do anything.
I sang the song
I had been given
& knew nothing.
The song gave me courage
to know something was meant
& that was the first thing I knew.
Turned north.
Now on the ground again as I was,
my hunger began to come back.
Turned south. There is a doubt
in any direction. That business
of the horns was scaring me now.
What kind of person had I become?
South had always been my sense of bad.

Not go south. I turned around again
& went through the little town,
keeping away from the square hole
that somehow kept attracting me,
I belonged there, or it belonged to me.
Got past it, eventually
got out of town. The road
was flat & empty again,
those low trees with big ones
further back. At least I could rest
in the woods. Elderberries.
Found them growing just off roadside,
profusely, ate & ate.
Something to go on. Back on the road
I kept going, walked on the crown
& did not veer. Far away
a car was coming towards me.
It was the Buick. I did not
feel like running away.
They stopped, & put me in,
this time in the back seat
I guess because I was filthy.
They continued south
a quarter-hour, came to a big
barbed-wire fence, with many
gaps torn in it. They now
dragged me out, pushed me
towards this fence. I was being
dumped back over the border
after all. Beyond the fence
I could see the edge of the marsh
where the railway ran, I could find
my way home. I said to the men,
I dont understand. The driver
pulled out a little book,
a traveller's phrasebook, slowly

& hard to figure out read this
to me: Your song
was not exactly wrong,
not a lie. But it is not
either the truth.
It took you
as far as it could.

I crawled through the fence
& within an hour
had reached the tracks again,
followed them down
again being careful
on the trestles
to where my car
was hidden, still safe,
the keys secure
under the rear cushion.
It started & took me home.
How could any song be wrong?
I kept asking.
And ask it still
when I look out of my room
& watch the maples
cast their shadows
in that slow arc around
that means a day.

# 24

I mean to have a natural way with things.
To go with them.
                    A way my father
would like, would have liked
to see me grow to, using hands & skills.
But his skill has always
taken me over, song, the way he did sing,
& does a little still, his voice
gone down to baritone, the pure note
he so loved, purissimo bel canto
failing in his seventy-second year.
The name of God
is spelt with the years of our lives,
my God has thirty-six letters, Lammed
Vav, is a Just Man,
                    a Good Man.
That I would want to be good. To skill
still after my father's music, he
lifting the song.
                    Our lives make God.
Can a man be good?
                    (If he takes his time,
goes slow with her, finds her pleasure
in his time, shapes
                    himself towards her,
relaxing even
                    into the form
grows out of her energies.
To which I have need

only to respond.)
                    Can a man
be good?
Go back to meat.
                    Now in my mind
an animal crumples to the ground
& breaks open, blue sac
of gut spills out, pale musclefibre
blueveined, liver & spleen
soaked in blood, the gut
slits, the greenish brown
half-digested world inside
goes back to the world. A look
of disengagement fills
the animal's eyes. I will not
specify it. Linnaeus
knows it not.
                    The song
          goes back to meat.


I will stand up & sing for my father.
A little snotnose kid, afraid
of what's up women's dresses,
                              afraid
of everything.
                    Pneumonia, drowning,
snakebite, fever, razor, fall
& precipice, mother I have not
learned to love I know you
in many way places,
mother E & mother D
holding your single
hand to my throat,
carotid,
          I would throw you
off. But my own mother

285

was of kind
& spared me
what she could,
                    never persuaded me
that the ordinary
was what was meant, I thank her
    & my father for his song,
compared with which
I must insist
my version's graceless —
but not for lack
of uncles & aunts
reposing out there,
Catholic, Protestant, Mason & nothing,
in the peaceful scary world
of ordinary things.
                    That
I would come to now natural,
au naturel, them & me
all naked
            in the fact of knowing
(being known).
                    Mahler, Symphony No.2,
c minor. Auferstehen.
                        An easter
in the autumn of the heart.
What Secret Power
Did These Men Possess?
Parasites. A hank of angels
knotted in their hair, a plug
of devils up the ass
& everything safely divided
into what they could & what they couldnt.
(& nobody else either). But I do,
must do, must force myself
over the inertia of the system

to perform. Only the impossible
               is any use.
Tyranny. Vagus nerve. To have done
with the judgment of man.

A blonde equestrienne
somewhat schiz
comes riding down
the bridle-path, mon coeur
at her stirrup, her post,
her little up & down, the
dancing in the Bois,
               the girl
on horseback, paradigm
of a whole mess of trouble.
What is that I spy between her
thighs is it an animal?
The Mounted God. The Aryan
Goddess making grief
for my black heart,
               o river!
But who am I to complain?
I have admired Jefferson so long
I'm ready for the trap,
               the simple
mechanism, labor-saving
device denominate: the Heart.
That it pumpeth. And what it
pumpeth, no man knoweth.
Not even Harvey, bathing
his gouty feet in the polarized
light of La Moon.
               *Le* Moon
I would insist, if I had
a place to stand —
               but she rides me down,

I have to duck, roll
away from the hooves,
hide in the gulley beside
in proximitate stercoris.
Up to my eyes in shit,
vegetarian at least, I'm the only
carnivore in this paradise,
in ventro equino.
To be calm
in face of the process
naturing me
all day long.

       Thistle
in my mouth I cry:
O Great Blonde Lady
I have no appetite
for your heel,
my mother bore me not
to crawl
upon the dungy ground,
I am your proper master
by the strength of my purpose,
get your brassy self just
down from that animule
I mean that horse
whose legs appear
even as I speak to you
to number seven
how can that be
get down get down.

A speech of that length
carries her out of earshot
so I brush the horseshit
off my person & trudge after,

confident that her feet
will touch earth again
or if we're both lucky
she'll land on my earth
precociously, victim
of the whimful hoss.
So that:
            in an eighth
of a mile I find her
serene while the horse
nibbles. She's still
seated, she watches
the gelding browse
as if she had nothing
better in the world
to do. I cry out as I
come near, –Be mindful
of corpses rotting
in the ditches of war,
recall the sweltering
east side morgue,
you too must have known
pain. –Sir, she replied,
I know nothing
of any matter you propose.
Unhand my ankle.
–But I have come
to master you
& incidentally
to replace
your thigh-companion
with something better
so get down & walk
beside me, your head
a head lower than mine
I mean let me look

down on you for once
& all of this mind
of yours will change.
–I think that too
is mine (she said)
to choose or decline.
This steed of mine's
no symbol of frustrate
maidenly zeal, it is
(look closely) none
but a horse, however
many legs you think to
number. Who asked you
to count my horse?
–Get down you rotten bitch
up there sedate on your soft
flesh I cannot bear
your elevation let me rise
to you let me tear you
down you are so far
away, you sit there
inside yourself I cannot bear
your distance & your
comfort in it, get down
& humble yourself
to my superior cunning
& strength of resolve.
I have been lonely
too long, I need you,
my work & its intention
begin to corrupt, I rot
apart from you, descend,
I am at the peril
of warp, deflection,
if I veer
my declination

will be on your head.

She tapped me with her crop
& cantered off, stopped
& looked back. –By nature
I am prone to ride & you
to walk. Your business
recruits you to the earth.
I keep my distance. That
is the law, the natural,
since you believe in nature.
If you were smart
you'd pull me down –
but if I once touch
earth I'll be no help
to you – or would I?
You'll never know –
Besides, my father
is a power in this town.

She rode off.
I watched her ass
bouncing on the saddle,
then when she passed
from sight I watched
the horse's ass
on the contrary most
stable, stepping
firmly. They both
blurred out soon
& I was left
to admire the
distances
that swallowed them up.
And to watch my step
since it was the only

game left to me
in this one-horse
town. Seven legs.
For Wisdom hath an house
of seven legs,
a glad heart lasteth
all the day
& sure there would be
other women in the park.
That's where I was wrong.
From that moment forth
not even a shadow
cast a curve — I wandered
howling in the desolate
male-reeking monkey-house
this jungle this urban
park this city this
phallic body this imp this
boy of grace
humping out between my
thighs. O lord
but it is lonely.
Down in here.
Send her down again
& I'll be sweeter,
or fiercer, or quicker,
or something else
flavored with sun &
raisins, buzzing with
bees & win her
to walk with me.


The pale sweet acid
green grapes, the sharp
persuasion of the taste,

or clean, that they bring
me back, unnatural,
not a seed inside them,
a handiwork, a triumph
over some nature
I have hardly imagined.
Clean song. A light voice
accurately lifted up,
proclaiming the note
dead on pitch.
What will kill me
is the adequate. Any life
I have is to refuse
to make do.
                Encounters
with women.
The insolent silence
they punish me with.
The abrasions of number.
Count, & count again.
The cunt is one,
                though some men
know her by a different number.
Mother Earth & Mother Death
your pool
drowned me in Wayne County,
your copperhead
bit me in Pike. My lungs
filled with your pus
in Brooklyn. In Queens
I found myself strangely
on a high coping
ready to fall, not knowing
how I came there.
                In your rain
I fell. On your wet leaves

the car spun round
three times in your honor
& threw us off the road.
I stood on the bridge
over the Harlem
cursing my life.
Am I to believe
that these marvels
of my ineptness or
strokes of fate
are instructive
of a unity
beyond my fear or
despair of life?
What anything means
is to go on.
To be alive
is an excuse to talk.
To sing the song
given to me
& hope to go on.
To get the note right
if there is such a thing.
To know the answer
to an absent question.
To skill.

# 25

The still-life.
A woman's painting
we have taken
into our house.
It illustrates
an accusation.
It entitles us
to no more favor
than the bottle, the grapes,
the flowers, the bright
cloths of Matisse
darkened in dream
of a blue woman,
her tits very prominent —
her presence
jeopardizes
the Still-Life —
but this woman
is not living,
          nature morte,
her hand)
     her hand
is already green, the light
shows through it,
what does that mean,
shadows spill
between her mind,
the frill of goldgreen light:
a thought
emanates

her dark world.
The fruit the flowers the table
the cloths. All nature
rehearses its parts,
prepares
to be a still life
in a mad mind,
            a blue
woman with most
prominent breasts she
painted, insisting
on the identity:
            a woman,
big tits.
       Whose dream
is she lost in now?
The light is broken
on an edge, that is,
the sun is broken,
did you know that?
The woman's painted
body arises like mist,
lower parts have
no definition
but the twist of loins
to signify lust.

A lust to be
as these objects are
fills her,
natural as they are
& no more
moving in the light of the lamp.

Over the meniscus of earth
rim of the white sun

going down
on all the colors.
I read in this her resolve
to have done with chances
& be an object,
            to be (it is sad,
a little kind) in someone's
hands —

since I & every other man
have failed her.

The accusation
itself
        entraps me,
I go to prison
in the dark of its connections —
as rich as the colors are
they all depend
on stone shadows for their depth,
orange has gaps in it
through which
some sort of descent. Oubliette.
All the things
she could never forget
gnaw at me.
            The city
does not get into the picture
except as shadows / fear / the light
gone out of the river
                    down there
& no one comes to her door.
The loneliness of what is not yet
prepared to call itself Love.

Meantime the birds

have gotten into my sleep
to grab the seeds, the bad
grains I am not supposed
to be supposed to eat. Wing
shade. Clobber
(clabber) behind the eyes
(between the brows).
                  Step by step
the objects illegitimately
discovered in the painting
transfer themselves
into my head. I am punished
by the Devils of Interpret —
let the woman go free.
Towngate on my shoulders
I call out to dark father
to throw me loose
with one toss of the dice —
I have never been a gambler,
preferring the realer risks
of what I do
              all day long,
the jeopardy of night
& what it brings to mind.
But now I would call out
to an earlier incarnation,
operatic, hidden
in glens, magnesium flares
specifying faces, Robert
le Diable, the gambler,
always trapped
between the woman
he is Fated
& the woman he thinks
himself to want,
              who goes to the altar

as a man climbs a mountain
hoping to fall off,
                    gamble,
to throw the dice
into the wager
of a wedding.
                A chance.
A throw of chances,
three 6s, called *Venus*,
come 6, come
extend your lordly 5
by the power of my One
into an agreeable sleep.
Wet dream.
.               The woman,
destitute of other chances,
throws herself.
How she falls.
There on the bed,
the way her arms
are pointing, are her legs
spread open or not,
if so, how much,
are her eyes open,
is she a little on her side
or flat on her back
or hiding
                —she throws
but he reads.
I read.
        The gambler begins
by accepting the situation.
He accepts her
as an object—the goal
refines itself in his mind:
he has a chance again

& how to bring
his number in.
What good are sixes now?
Theodora weeps
because she cant
take men in
by any hole
beyond her three;
she cries
let her nipples
open
& make the five,
let her heart
open to be six.
But no man
had such a cock
could fuck her heart.
Her heart closed
& stayed that way.
The Empire froze
into bank rates,
the chance fell
out of her body
& became a coin,
vomited its gold,
supposed its valor
to be the emperor's
will to make it worth
whatever that sleepless
cunning jovial man
could constellate
as compensation
for Theodora's pain —
if she couldnt take in
utterly,
                she'd love no more

& rule by death
which leaves no fraction,
no hole unfilled.
Pays all debts.

The gambler
will not settle for this dream.
He knows a woman
has been silenced, stuck
in the posture
she fell in when he left,
when he did not answer.
He throws a burning hedge,
a circle of tricky fire
done by the mirrors
in his head, the flares
of his intermittent
intelligence. He starts up
the mountainside
but slides back down.
He throws a tomb
where she lies
self-poisoned for his sake.
Her ghost appears
& tells him No
that is too easy —
my life is shadow
but I live still.
He hears her, doesnt
want to, grinds
his teeth, snaps
his lucky thumbs & fingers,
throws again:

A ship that brings her back,
this time

she comes to him,
he need exert no effort,
it's a cherry fallen
into his mouth, she does it all,
she draws the wind
to belly out the sail,
she is naked on the prow
she leaps ashore
—but he doesnt know
what more to do.
He runs to fuck her,
gladly, understanding that,
she takes him in
& when they rest apart
she looks at him.
Immense demand.
Moved for one
fraction by love
he turns & rides
the vector of her glance
& sees himself
as she, in her moment,
wills to see him.
If he accepts that vision
he must act.

       But he gets
up on his knees,
rolls the dice again.
A city
falls on his back
& he carries it
patiently, it does not
talk to him,
he does not have to
answer it,

it is quiet,
it just hurts,
           it lumps
him down, he is strong,
he carries the city
looking for a gate
to stow it behind,
finds nothing, the city
keeps growing, the pain
is bearable. History
was never much different.
He goes along.
He is doing this
for me,
           out of the strength
of our genetic union,
because of something
I have failed,
an answer I did not give
in any sense,
           in any senses.

Or else why the reproach
of her black corridors of paint,
the big blue tits
that look so enormous
up the perspective of the hall,
her smaller body
waiting at the final door.
Or the postcard I get:

"and the name of the star is called Wormwood:
and the third part of the waters became worm-
wood; and many men died of the waters, because
they were made bitter."

Woman!
That your revelation
is always revenge!

I did not lay the traps
you found your way to,
I looked away
as you walked in, not mine
to tell you where to walk,
I looked away. I made it
none of my business,
doubting all the while in my heart
your capacity to hear me,
to answer me
exactly. We turned
from each other in each other.
Maybe. Maybe.
                    There was no part
of you that could hear me.
Therefore I did not speak.
And therefore, Mara, Amara,
Maria, Miryam, Ama, sterile
woman,
            you turned the ocean
to wormwood, your beauty
made me thereafter drink,
a third
        part of me died.
I detect the stench of my parts
in the coffin of your painting,
your poem, your scribbled
desperation
            that's still less
desperate than the parts
of me that remain
                to read you.

To take a chance again
& one day try to speak to you
with customary optimism
while all of us are secretly
busy all day long
mourning our dead,
the questionless answer
I gave you so freely
in the full of daytime,
the answerless questions
you probed me with all night.
We mourn the hour
when those things meant so much.
And now the terror
waits in the painting, in the reproach
I am strangely
willing to read there,
November among men.

# 26

Not doubt.
The story
picks itself up
& moves out.
Hallway
from apartment
to john,
dark enough
to run naked
as they did.
Way down in
the coffin-
shaped notch
of sunlight:
the door.
The street
ran through
every room.
Nothing
was far.
She hunched
down
in the corner
made sure
she was pressed
against both
walls, the floor,
she reduced
the space

occupied.
She was small.
In different
directions
things
were coming
at her
slowly
giving her chance
to choose or
forget.
In the city
everything is
slow — people
hurry towards her
but the actual
speed is low,
botanical,
she feels
groped for
a man
fumbles
in her wood,
where,
can he
find her,
that aromatic
resin that
leaf ooze
that turns
him so
on,
    her wet,
he looks
she does not
leak, I saw this

first
in the cellar
of that hungarian
house, looking
out, eye level,
window
to the peach tree
in the garden
halfway
to the vine,
the tree, the gum
came down
& caught the sun
later
in my hands,
the taste of it,
the peaches
we did not get,
the gum, the ooze
of a woman
I had not yet
discerned from
tree
    now she
turns into a door
& he hurries
upon her
hoping to turn her
also
to his doctrine
of entrances,
his funny
room, she is apart,
she has never
understood
what he is doing

at her, his
part,
     it follows her
down the hall
it is the key
shoved in
& twisted
till she screams,
the door
will yield
she will
not give in,
she ceases
to be wood,
takes refuge
in iron. An age
must pass
before he learns
to smelt —
by then
her hair is copper
in some lights,
she lay
among the maple
leaf, mounds, autumn,
rare trip
up river
worked down
among the leaves
hoping
invisible.
He finds.
The elixir
reeks now
at the end of
all his points,

she has a choice
no element
can resist him
so she turns
into silence
& passes in
between his teeth,
gap teeth, he'll
never find her
there, he breathes
her out
& she is nowhere
but secure
from his usages.
*I reached in so deep*
*I could never find bone —*
the song
fluttered away from him,
lost him
not hard
for a good
man to find work.
Other town.
Exit.
    Now what
is she trembling
about now now
what now is she now
trembling like a now
in the lap of cold
now she chose now
to be so & now
no other way to
be now.
       She is a hall
in my memory.

She is naked
because men look at her.
I looked at her
& she was naked
as agreed,
        his song
remembers her.
Remember me
to remind her.

The hall was dark.
Keyhole
filled with sun
or something
saying it was sun
did you believe
I did not ask
it was enough
to remember.
It is not enough to remember.
Her skin
wallpaper
imprinted
by my habits
of attention
such as they
are attentions
to her skin
imprinted
by what I have
decided
her body to say
say it/sing it to me
& other familiar
neglects. The hall
sharpened

at its distal end
with light
ripped her open
every time she
tried to go out
when she got
to the street
she was wasted,
wasted, her eyes
for all their
humors
      dry
from a continuous
sleep.
      Her voice
caresses us both still.
It is lovely
& agreeable
to my furthest
suspicions
of a lust
rising in me
to tend towards.
Warning given.
To scream it:
*I was the house*
& she obsessed
my narrow places
as with an army
of casual
militiamen
aching for dawn
& how to go home,
warriors
of a mistake.
*I was the house*

& how could she go?
She recalled
her smile
from the lips,
her breath
was sweet
even for a moment
in my hand.
Her tongue went in
& I held it.
The whole city
was a surprise.
Snipers,
         at least.
Call
for a commune
in which this skin
takes on a work
different at last
from me just
looking at it.
Heals both of us?
Or none. Or some
other one, elsewhere,
some other time.
*I was the house*
& she ran
along my hallway
to the bathroom,
back
to the apartment
full of greasy
dishes & dirty
clothes, all politesse
thrown off
& never washed,

too naked
to remember.
And then I remember
I am dreaming this
out of the actual
fact.

      I mean the fact
has its own dream,
we live it out.
It masses us
on the borders
of an experience.
It is not imagination.
The fact
mobilizes us
to a dance
so antic
we call it war
& suppose
it the most factual
of all our distortions.
She sings me,
sometimes.
It is not enough to remember her song
clipped out of my song boiled
out of the clothes
I had hoped she would
neglect to wear. She did,
or didnt, the hall
filled regular
with ordinary light,
what could be better,
she ran
from any like me,
the stamens

of agression
were not for her,
the bee
could suck itself
for all she
cared & I cared
to talk to her
again & again,
delighted I suppose
by the soft silence
I got myself
to take for something
sexier than speech.
A lisp
as if some honey
came between our
lips, not made there
but found there,
a wilding,
a revolutionary
touch.

The flags
went up
the moon fell down
& the country
of our conviction
split in half,
I shared a river
with her washing
her clothes for her
in my head
so that the stones
would get into it
I hoped she would
learn to become.

Not a machine
but a bone,
           just a little
that we could get outside
the house we guessed
was on our minds.
                 I have
a snapshot
of her among it,
only her eyes
vertical
in all that fall.
I reached in so deep I
never found
bone I tried
& all the rest
was the simplest light.

# 27

Two friends I love
& left them
over the hill
while I gathered
cones from my own tree.
Burnt them
for my only light,
hymenaie, hymenaie,
the wine
in the rhyton
has to be drunk
all in one drink,
the cup has no base,
wont stand, is a horn
with grinning
devil head
I drink from his lips,
exactly
my reflection in the
glimmering red wine.
Green wine of vitriol,
it is so simple
now I changed
my mind,
   I drink
from my own lips
also,
  I have grown
so kind I know

how to do that,
a drink,
or leave it alone,
outwoods, pile
of birch sawdust
where they found
the poor man's
daughter,
a winter mystery
recalled from summer.
The putrefactions,
o I used to think
along them,
a mind like a nose,
& then
at the attended moment
in the intense work
it all turned yellow,
my fingers
white with power
how tight I squeeze.
How can a woman
stand it,
the weight, the pression,
the hammer
when the work
is not dark
& it's all
out there,
in the beautiful
street again.
Be with me
while it breaks in two
& half is street
& half that
music leads us

companionably down
into & out
of our own clefts,
to the real vulva,
the evergape,
the place I am going.

I hear Delius now & it reminds me I want to
sleep. Want to gentle in a bed, alone, listen to
the wind coming across the Verdugo Mountains
on the other side of the music. West wind.

Today
our first
sight of the
sea (the road
was no different,
a band
of light,
white
of my eye)

Or what do I see when I look in the cup. Cer-
tainly my own face bobbing & trembling, the
color of desire & it is true I see Desire as wearing
this face. A party of Arikaras counting coups. A
band of dirty monks looking for Egypt, lost in
my perineal spaces, convinced they have come to
hell & here the Devil rules with groan & torture
& malevolent images distorted from what they
fancy to be the good. The good is yucca. Believe
me. The good is that fifteen-foot scape cocking
up above the desert once its life & flowering.
Gets up high enough so that when it dries & falls
the seed-head, the honeyhead, hits the ground at
the right distance from the parent bush, gets a

chance, out there, in Deserto. The monks open
their prayer books, & each capital letter I have
rubricated with a naked woman, line drawing
(more seductive than a hint at texture), a wo-
man-shaped gap for their eye to espy, fall upon,
fall through, change their minds. Red lines to
draw a woman. Blue lines, blue veins throbbing
on the white shaft. To marry the colors, in inter-
change.


And even sometimes
I want to be alone.




November 15$^{th}$.
Strong wind,
temperature 50°
in these hills.
To be naked
under the lemon tree
would be a puzzle.
The moonlight
gets lost in bamboo.
The work
has gone from black
to white
& to that yellow
we have detected
in some birds,
a finch,
that fine old
fuck-bird
who makes the summers,

late summers,
so full of noise
in Annandale,
the road down
Kidd's Lane
them sitting
on all the wires
a jump ahead
of the dry falls
the not so old bridge.
The snow is there now,
& Nona's last zucchinis
would be puckering,
best for playing
coarse sexual jokes
in the mood of finch
& the ass of October.
But now I prop
my eyelid open
& finally observe
that in this autumn
& hundreds of lives
into the day's book
the work
has turned white.
This morning Ted
saw a raven
fly over this house.
It did not stop.
It was flying
simply
away.
Because the process
has its colors
& those
are its precisions,

& I have known them
also
in the look
in Helen's eye,
the titrations of hunger
in my own
tossed back
by the full glass
lifted
less to quench thirst
than to estimate
my need.
The raven
has flown away,
the bad smell
has left the house,
the sewers
run to the sea,
we saw the sea today
boiling gold
under an opposite
sun,
  the house
knows a new odor,
like that musk
makes faint women faint
but not that smell,
or nearer
to the lemon,
the green
comes before yellow
but it is not permitted
to see the green,
only the Pacific today
across the basin,
the white

solidity
of the Light
when it finally,
whisk of wind
& glance of eye,
in the heart
of the most
meaningless act,
enters
the Matter.

The Waker: "What are you saying?"
The Sleeper: "I'm not talking to you."
The Waker: "But what were you saying anyhow?"
The Sleeper: "Nursing infant."
The Waker: "What about a nursing infant?"
The Sleeper: "It laughed when fed pepper."
The Waker: "What kind of pepper?"
The Sleeper: "What do you call it?"
The Waker: "Red?"
The Sleeper: "Yes, that's right."
The Waker: "Who were you telling it to?"
The Sleeper: "To my mind."

Here the Dreamer
most rarely
stands & speaks for itself,
interrupted
in its nightly work
of telling stories
to what it thinks of as
its mind. My mind.
And I woke
hours later
troubled that I had had
no dreams,

                    then Helen woke
& told me the dialogue
she had sustained
with some me beside her
early in my sleep.
See, the infant is born,
is laughing
& taking nourishment
from hot things.
The child is born
to red delight,
begins to know its mind.
The black of the womb
is over now.
The paleskin child
lusts for the red
he must become.
It must become.
This infant
has no sex yet
but will have every.
Wake up.
The definition
begins.

# 28

Guided by the clock
a little
lifted past my fears,
only a minute
& then the dread
will know itself again
maybe, & maybe not,
I reach.
Polymers.
A coat of gold
one molecule thick
along the nosecone,
introduction
to the cosmic world
where gold works
even on top of our tricks.
A map of Mars,
as if, as if that's
where we were heading
to flee the center.
And that *we*
is not impeccable,
I will not join it,
I will assert
now with the calm
face of Desire
that the Sun
is a climate
we will inhabit,

that the heat
is our relation
with it,
but not itself,
that the Light
knows itself
in another
condition
& we can walk there
in the cool
of evening.
The Sun was Eden.
East of it
the planets rise
more or less
eccentric,
sons flying
to the high places
& the drunken
comas of propagation
in which a man
doubts himself
& immediately
a specter rises
from his doubt,
a not-speak,
an infant.
In all the heavens
of insecurity
there is no molecule
deadlier than.
Because the Child
must be born
in confidence, in
ripeness, full.
And there is the history

of it all again,
the Child
of a conception
dour & austere
(born
out of my head)
supposed to leap
joyful,
            its heart
never circumcised,
gay as the
doubt is long —
failed child,
you will be
born at last.
Every womb
has a way of its own.
You spill.
You are agreeable
when the wine
goes down.
Paracelsus:
How to make Homunculus.
How can I translate
back into street,
people walking
because they like to
& all the windows
full of chance?

Second Movement:
the power
of a beginning
examines itself.
It is slow.
The conductor

wants to make it dance.
OK, it dances.
What does it matter,
nobody's listening.
She falls
over her feet
her legs go up,
their eyes
run up her legs
as casual
as shadows of
leaves falling.
Their glances
land in her crotch
& see nothing
but mountain there,
all the salt
in the mountain
long ago hacked out
& carted down
by muleteams
to a populous
valley.
Hunger for salt.
Boron. Chloride.
These are towns,
substances
discerned
in the unlikely
places, in deserto,
she sits on the curb
& remembers.

The rocket
comes down
through the new

atmosphere, We're here,
we're here,
she looks up
& considers
our arrival,
-Why did you take
so long,
            was it
you
      afraid
of my young
power now
cold into
is it memory?

Hard to hear her,
she is younger
than our journey,
on earth
would be jailbait
with dangerous lips
& interested
in anybody's story.
-O maid of Mars
(I addressed her)
can we play
on your street?
It is so long
since I tasted salt,
my name is Robert,
I am a ranger from
a continent called
the Civil War,
if I were water
I would lap your feet.
She hugged her knees

as I supposed she would,
& smiled a princely
welcome to her deficit.
I am Wasted, she said,
I have been here so long
I cant get started
& other old songs.
You can have me
if you want me
but we'll all have
to get away,
the time of this
planetary cycle
is over I think,
it has to do
with Venus, & people
who went there
from your country
before your kind
got there, that's what
the old man told me
& all he really wanted
was to get
inside me,
in that doorway
before the people went
& left me here
with the memory only
of their glances,
their attitudes
to keep me warm.
-It's plenty warm
(I said)
where I am,
let's go together
wherever it is.

-Is that all you
want of Mars,
just to pick a
girl up
in the last street?
I'll come with you
though I surely wish
you were somebody else.
-Who?
            -It doesnt
matter, only
somebody more
into geography
than you are.
I'm only a part
of the lay of the
land, I mean it's
ok with me but
wouldnt you rather
fuck a whole
planet & not just me?
-I dont get you.

-You get me all right,
what choice do
either of us have,
you get me, but this
whole world
is empty, I was just
waiting for you,
whoever you
turned out to be.
I only got here
myself at the end
of their lives,
those Martians, you

should have seen them
packing into their
ship, a few
looking back at me
& wondering
how I'd make out.
Nobody offered to
take me along.
Take me along
if you want to,
I'm not proud,
I've been alone
too long.
       Other
old songs. We went
back into my
craft & hovered
a mile up on a nice
clear day.
The big crystals
of their armatures
flickered in sun,
a jackrabbit
hit a powerline,
we could see the flash.
-Jackrabbit, she said,
they're always
doing it. The dumb
Martians never bothered
to turn the thing off.
-What does it do?
-I never found out,
kills rabbits.
-When did you get here?
-Years ago, my mother
brought me, dont ask me

how. She played the cello
& hated me to ask
questions, that's how
I got so accepting.
-My name is Robert I said.
-You said that already.
-My name is Robert
I went on & I have come
to collect you —
I picked you out
from beyond the moons —
you are necessary
for a gathering I plan
of certain cosmic
personalities, entities
representative
of the best intelligent
(here what I was saying
got drowned out by a massive
hum from a shot transformer,
switched it off & went on)
life from earth, a company
of Love & Wisdom. -Now
you're talking, she said.
-I could tell you all their names
but the names dont do justice.
I could tell you the emblem
you'll get to wear,
& the colors of the dresses
chosen
for each day
of the heliocentric week —
but come with me & find
Out for yourself.
I chose you when
you stumbled & fell,

my eyes, with all
the others, went
between your thighs
& what I saw there
smelled sweet as a
river, a rain, a
chance for many nations
to begin again.
This time (I cried)
the Woman has fallen —
salvation
is seeing her.
In this world
the truest vision
of God is a, or is as a
beautiful woman –
so I came up here
to find you now
bring you
            to my garden.
-Which is where?
-Where all the others
have gathered,
come in their beauty
below the vine
stretched across
the hop-poles
at the door of my
kingdom.
            -Are you
a king, then?
-I am king
only of those
who have become
themselves.
-I saw your face once

reflected
from the tip of a needle.
-How sharp your eyes are,
but not sharp as mine –
I saw you
a planet away,
I saw you stagger
from the laundromat
& fall, I saw
your secret parts
when you sprawled
out on the sidewalk
& didnt care,
I saw them look at you
& saw
          what none of them saw,
that the life
of their planet
lay inside your
lips like an egg,
a globe of light
that dimmed
in proportion
as they did not
look at it.
You crawled
over to the curb
& sat there,
& in your heart
you were
waiting for me.
-Not just my heart.
I was hungry,
horny, I wanted to bear
what I felt inside me
out in the world.

-So I hurried,
before you sat an hour
I had descended,
the gold
anodized upon
my eyelids helped
me find you.
Now I take you
if you will
to be taken.
-Go ahead, take me,
stop pretending
I have some kind of
choice. Take me.
-Then you admit
this is not Mars
any longer, this
earth you've seen
leave you one last time?
-I admit it, it's just
a boring desert town,
they've all
gone away.
And this is your car,
on the Barstow Freeway,
get moving, I cant
stand the suspense.
If it werent
for my mother's training,
I'd be wearing us both out
with questions. Just
let's get going.

All this while
the car'd been idling,
along the roadside

a few tracks led
off into sand, salt
desert. Now that I had her,
where should we go?
I drove south,
towards the San Gabriels
hoping the nearness of
my house would teach me
where exactly
it was I left my garden.
She talked about some
days of her experience.
I listened
& thought fast.
-Listen, I told her,
listen, I am alone.
I have no kingdom
but myself.
The vines & the props
are heavy with grapes,
the wine
pools out in shadow,
there is enough in me
for everyone.
Listen to me.
There is a wine
pressed from distance,
drink it with me
in my kingdom,
I am only a garden
& its idle gardener,
the trees
do all the work,
the grasses lift
a little beyond
the dry earth

by their own power,
my power
is to know these things,
& feel them,
                here
(I touched her
under her nearer breast),
I sit up on the hill
& listen,
the company I told you of
addresses me all night,
it is not lonely,
the roots go down
& I will talk
to you forever.
She was silent
in the face
of that deception
which loved her
better than truth.
In her silence
I found
another kind of garden
& with it
the ugliness
of the image of a
garden,
                not
to guard it, not
to enclose,
but this whole
freeway linked
to the space
it seemed to
violate
but in fact

revealed.
Apocalypse.
Nothing is profane.
Her heart was distant.
I noticed that my hand
still lay under her
breast where it had
worked itself in,
dormant, not seeking
to arouse. I wondered
if she would speak.
Her heartbeat
was slow, regular, unlike
what I supposed
it would be doing
with all that stuff in her.
She spoke: -I thought
you were Death
coming for me,
your Maiden,
& I would have given you
gladly
my last virginity.
But now I see
or think I see
that you're not Death,
you're something
much more complicated.
Maybe I could
get interested,
maybe not.
These deserts
may be groovy for you
but I'm sick of them
take me (since
you're taking me)

somewhere
with streets in it,
& people, jesus,
are there any
people left?
Her blues
were beginning to
get to me,
-It's not all that
sad, we're together,
the car is moving,
there is a city
over the mountains,
is that what you mean?
I was trying
to bring you to my garden,
I still believe in you
in it, you'll work there,
it will be more
than you ever bothered
to imagine.
                    -I'm sick
of this story
you keep imagining.
Dont lay all that
obligation on me
to live up to some
fantasy of me in your
garden. I hate flowers.
-It's not
that kind of garden.
-Then dont call it
garden — what a boring
word to use
for anything with
people in it.

-People havent treated
you so well.
-What else do I have?
I love the people
in me — that's all
that really matters.
-Everything I planned
encloses you.
You, like any woman, any
man, are caught
in the web of those who
see you. The people in town
did not see you when you fell —
I did. I saw
what you were hiding.
You are a victim of perception:
we belong
to those who see us best.
To this she made no answer
but watched the road intently
as if it brought her
a chance lost to me.
What was it? What
was she looking for?
We were in the mountains
before she spoke again,
only it wasnt speaking
but a dreary kind of humming
with words in it, crazy
but we were crazy together
& there was nothing to choose
between us, a madman
& his find, a girlwoman
from the other side,
the two of us, all
too much at home in mountains,

she was humming
something about rabbits
& crying, she was coming
down, the turns in the road
were tricky & I soon
took my hand from her breast.
-It cant end like that
(I said), you cant just go
drooping, silver-crazy,
the moon all over your mind
& dripping from your eyes.
I'm going somewhere
& you're going with me.
There's no other way.
She didnt answer
but she did stop humming,
her eyes dried
in the desert wind.
She faced nowhere
& after a while
looked glad about it.
At that stage
I pulled the car
into a turn-out
& the whole thing
rested. -Forgive me,
I said. -It was
nothing, she said.
The whole time got
away from us, it wasnt
really your fault.

We walked out
on one of those rocky
elbows tricky
with loose soil.

She spotted a bush
with red flowers
growing twenty feet down
a fairly steep slope,
slid down to it, picked
one little flower, a bell
or trumpet, put it in her
mouth & kicked her way
back up. -How many years
have to pass
before this makes sense?
she asked me
& I took the flower
from her mouth
with mine. This passed
for an intimacy
but nothing followed.
If only I had not been
coated with gold
& she with silver
the electricity
that passed between us
would have meant something —
but there it was, running
in the mountains, dimetallic,
going off into the air.
As if the air
needed it. The current
was for our sake
& we couldnt use it.
It would have been better
not to get started.
Maybe the bush
would flourish better
because we'd been there.
Maybe not. I wanted a sign

& what we had
was each other
but not much.
I wanted a sign
& I still had the crumpled
flower in my teeth,
I took it out
with my fingers
& rubbed it on her cheek.
-We have to try, honey,
we have to try to do it.
-Yes, I know what you mean.
Just because it doesnt matter.
Whatever happens,
it's just itself, the same
as itself, nothing
different. We have to try,
dont we?
            I drove us
to a motel. We went in
& did it. It wasnt much fun
so we did it again.
The hours pass. I slept
& woke to find a note from her:
        "Everything is the
        same as itself,
        what else could it be?
        You wanted me to mean too much —
        that made you old & me young,
        & that's terrible.
        Or the other way around.
        Take care of yourself,
        & maybe another time.
        This is the longest
        letter I've ever written.
        You were right about the garden,

when I'm ready you'll find me there.
But you'd better have something
definite in mind.
Or maybe you werent.
I'm not sure. But I get restless
waiting around.
But I will be.
And you better.
The worst part is
it's always like this
isnt it. Or I guess
love is not enough.
Or where do you *need* it?
I'm not sure about me."

# 29

The wind
last night
& now
raga,
a modal phrase
of Bruckner
terrifying
played
by what chance?
on the sarod,
a beginning.
Cosmology
carried
(trembling
in every limb)
into the schools,
Paralysis Mundi,
Palsy of the World.
Predicaments:
five in the morning
cockcrow,
coyote howl.
A word in the mail.
The animal
rimes with the bird.
In both their cases,
dawn.
What the wind did:
a branch of the big tree down.

The deciduous bush
stripped bare.
The flowers: no change.
They're always strongest,
strange
they should be thought delicate,
generative parts.
Guarded groin.
                    What the wind
meant was harder to say.
So dont say it. Remember
the 7$^{th}$ proposition
in the *Tractatus*,
have at least that
much decency
in a secular world.
Pleonasm. The wind
says it & says it again.
Alicja, her cheeks rounding
strangely in pregnancy.
We fall
into each other's hands.
The wind.
                    Predicaments:
It shakes. It goes down
& comes again. It rises
wherever it likes.
The wind
is always three,
toujours, your skinny
legs on the Common
stretched out crazy
for the wind, not the sun,
no sun in Boston,
the river
has its number, that's all

five. Years away.
Magazine Beach. Demoiselles
of Despair, I know you
in your dark apartments.
Maybe a marriage
alternates with silence.
                              Changes
nothing. The wind
is still master of his house,
& o what he did to our
garden. Where do you put
a tree branch
when it's fallen
still full of leaves?
Lift it up a little?
Raise it
arms length
to sky,
        & if so, in
testimony or reproach?
Where do you put a leaf?
Leave it
for the gardener.
Then who am I?
Dunno. You're somewhat
to do with the weather.
Well, wind up
your horoscope
& come with me. That noise
is a tomb breaking open,
the people coming out
beyond the gates, the gates
torn down, o god, there are
people on both sides of the gate,
everywhere
is the land of our possibility.

Predicament:
to be free.
(Sustained applause.) Free
in the wind.
(Old Song.)
Predicament: to be free
& not to believe it
is worse than chains.
Look who's talking,
you who have become
the armor you are.
What can I do
with a piece of tree?
Plant it? Dim crafts
of gardeners, grafting,
slipping, the maiden
buggered near the altered
tree, the woman who tends
the fields, her girdle
loosed, walks round
trailing her clothes.
Against the pests
who come to gnaw
this peaceful dinner,
this mild, this aequo animo
possession, this field.
O Body
stronger than time,
stronger than all the names
I knew you by,
defend my ground.
Only the place I stand,
to know her
& to talk
a little lifted
from the ordinary

& then fall back.

Clouds now cover the sun.
A different
dispensation
of the light.
Nea Diathêkê.
The leaves
all over the ground.
What good are they?
Mulch. Compost.
The arcane gardener
oils his tools.
I go out to look at the sky,
come back with a rose.
Heavy clouds coming in
from the Pacific, blue sky
over the mountains:
between them, a light like
Good Friday
shivering the earth,
rending the veil.
                    The rose,
a pale salmon, rosier
at the tips of petals,
color of light
passing through flesh,
Goethe's *rose-purple*,
glow of flashlight
in fingers.
                    To smell
red roses
strengthens the nerves:
who said that?
Thin pulse, I feel
thin as paper, the rose

restores my dimensions,
how many? I wake in heaven.
And know these things
not by the book,
*Rose, you pure gainsaying,*
*lust*
*to be no one's sleep*
*under all those eyelids.*
But that's the book,
& the thorn
is still in my thumb,
the feel of it.
To strengthen the nerves,
dissolve the memory.
Alicja, pale winter in Poland,
walks by the huge tall window.
Into Dorothy, dropped
from what cadenza
into Kansas, canyon, crater
of affection, loud voices
of beerdrinkers, into the meadvat,
the old metheglin, the beer
on her chin, the smile —
to dissolve that
into the rose.
And there's only the rose.
I mean a flower,
picked
a few days after its peak,
just after the new moon.
From this garden,
a leggy not
very productive rosebush
against the white fence,
the hills behind it
populated, not mystical,

magicked only
by the will of those
who walk there,
if they have magic, if their wills
work this afternoon
when the light looks
as if it's all been said.
The sun comes out.
The spider on the rose
I put back to the bush,
not wanting to interfere
more than I had to
to steal the rose.
Which technically
belongs to me. O technê!
O techniques
of owning & possession!

"You see it is the people who generally smell of
the museums who are accepted, and it is the new
who are not accepted. You have got to accept a
complete difference. It is hard to accept that, it
is much easier to have one hand in the past."

Predicament:
to be a spider
on a rose
some hand wants to pluck.
To want a rose.
To go into the museum
where it is always
quiet. Dorothy's
blue highheels
stuttering forward
on the marble floor.
Among the dead

where such life
has a poignance
I could hardly stand,
Lois's shadowed eyes,
researchers
who could call me
to life.
Rosepetal
on the marble,
tracked in
with rainy feet,
the mud. The snow
on white marble
at Williamstown,
rainy sky
over Fécamp,
a naked woman
back to us
moving into the forest.
Predicament:
that every
thing moves,
moves me,
can move. Or must move.
Wrench of the arbitrary,
realigning the gears
of the monster museum,
the silence that waits
for every labor.
Not even a giggle
can be lost.
They lock us in at night.
At Christmas
the snow falls
on David Smith's steel
& the forms

belong to no one.
But the books
pin them down.
Antipygmalion.
Women made into statues,
wax museum, the glue
replaces blood,
the bees
          cohabit,
exit male, the bees
lock their honey
in geometry,
              nothing
stands free. Rhodomel.
Rose thorn & honey
spined with intelligent
wardens, all lost,
all locked
away in the airless room.
It locks.
My head is slow.
Cock crows.
It changes
into the liberty
of light.
Allowed to hope again
I wonder how to
melt the bronze.
Or melt the Brahms
congealed in floral
patterns, a museum
of honey, sweet
as arithmetic.
Numbers mounting
towards a sexless
paradise

where no man's body
means a thing
                or no
body walks.
Sweet without salt,
dying city,
                as if the rose
were only its smell.
The nerves
do not live on sugar.
Potassium
never at rest,
dark Kali, red
Kali,
        burn
of her unfenced
energy,
                this substance
will not let
the world be
ordinary.
                She touches
everything.

The garden.

At last.

What the wind
left.
What I remember
enough
to lift.
The garden
is soft,
depends
on the crustal

instability
that makes the mountains.
It is a rift
in other people's matter.
Heart attack.
Earthquake.
Quiet place, a door
opens on it —
to make love there?
Love has
no need of that,
a long time
since love's
been in a garden,
hortus conclusus,
or any garden
but herself,
soma, the body
I would charm
to live with me.

"Spearmint,
Rew, will hardly grow
Fetherfew prospereth exceedingly;
Southernwood, is no plant for this Country, Nor
Rosemary, Nor
Bayes.
White-Salten groweth pretty well, so doth
Lavender-Cotton.  But
Lavender is not for the Climate
Penny Royal
Smalledge.
Ground Ivey, or Ale Hoof
Gilly Flowers will continue two years.
Fennel must be taken up, and kept in a Warm
            Cellar all Winter,

Horseleek prospereth notably
Holly hocks
Enula Campana, in two years time the Roots rot.
Coriander, and
Dill, and
Annis thrive exceedingly, but Annis Seed,
        as also the seed of
Fennel seldom comes to maturity; the Seed
        of Annis is commonly eaten by the fly.
Celary never lasts but one Summer, the Roots
        rot with the Frost.
Sparagus thrives exceedingly, so does
Garden Sorrel, and
Sweet Bryer or Eglantine
Bloodroot but sorrily,   but
Patience and
English Roses very pleasantly.
Celandine by the West Country now called Kenning
        Wort grows but slowly.
Muschater, as well as in England.
Dittander or Pepperwort flourisheth notably
        and so doth
Tansie."

How to live with me
in a cold country.
Transcendental flowers,
the sea below the lawn
& everything taking its time.
Day rhythm
conceding to be long.
Of a day : ephemeris
stars in her eyes?
                the gate
flaps in the wind
& lets the breeze

into the herb-garden
to disperse the scents,
untie the knot.
I go down twenty
years into the cellar
where I brought my friend
lacking a house,
                    peachtree
outside, cellar steps
gap in roughcast wall,
the four steps
to the sense of garden.
Coriander, whose seeds
are warm & leaves
most cold,
                two-time flower,
kiss him on the lips,
the last mouth
dares to know you.
Potassium,
or the need to love.
It is not naked
just to be in the garden
agreeing with the wind.
Kick
      the door down,
at last, o woman
where would I have brought you
to be so quiet,
I need you outwards.
Not the rose.
The roses of Shawmut,
Rosa rugosa
needs salt spray,
rocks,
      a cape in wind

a tongue out
at Europa,
                    no need, the seed
lives amongst us
& does not wander.
The seed
is in the wind.
Every condition
is to be out.
Yucca, the scape
uplifted, once in its life,
to get out.
To have for a while
no place to stand,
fall through air,
winged seed of maple,
dandelion fluff
across the seasons,
trying to get out.
You said
what the vast garden needed:
places to fuck in,
secluded, grass,
pine needles. I added
a fountain. To come there
make love & leave —
sense enough
to find in a garden.
Indian music
on the radio,
beginning to declare
its form,
                    a phrase
of Bruckner's
by that chance
I know as Play

& flees the garden.
Not garden,
yard,
the cellar steps
lead up to it,
it is not gracious,
things grow there,
it is
     outward
of a house
& towards forever.

*What grows by itself*
*is all that matters,*
yard & vacant lot,
railroad siding
from which accurate
seed is carried
in the belly
of an impeccable wind
past the gorgeous
garden of the cultivars,
over the intentions
of foresightful men
anxious to own,
into deserts
& hope for the best
or into this yard
either side
of no man's fence,
there is no gate,
it moves
& knowing it
would heal
all the diseases
of propriety,

the good taste
that ruined us,
we come to
in a world
self-planted,
the averroist seed
keeps coming down,
the pollen
comes into my head.
The wind
reminds me.

I have done
my flirtation
with vegetables.
Now the flesh
is its own fever,
'scarlet' to know
& blushing to care,
rubescent,
swollen & red
to touch,
not to take
possession
but to touch,
to get it in,
past the histamines
of aversion,
the warning glances,
the lepress's
heart
        painted on her tunic,
Sir John stands up
his one eye most
blind, his mouth
anxious to declare

the difference
between green & red.
The garden
shatters
in the moment
of my need.
The afterimage
of its organic forms
burns in my eye,
the red
lips
    that do not
know how to close,
the flower
opened forever.
After all the philosophies
of roses
to come to the wisdom
of thorn.
The spine
inside me
standing up
all my life,
around which curl
the red snakes of fire
& the blue
dragons of reception,
*to heal*
*is to hear.*
Suddenly it is clear:
only my eyes
have been trapped
in the garden.
When the walls fell,
only my eyes
were freed.

The wind
had been there
all the time,
sometimes mumbled
by the walls,
but I could always hear
beyond them,
where the breath goes
over the wall.
What's there?
A lawn.
What's growing?
"By itself."
Coriander hot & cold,
torsions
of red & blue
bodies, forms
entangled
in Desire Body,
this instrument
of grace.

So after the wind
one trunk of the
bush by the greenhouse
had come down.
I went at it
with the old axe,
split haft & rusted
head,
the red would not work
on the green wood,
went back
& got the saw
could get my arm in
under the boscage

to begin.  A few strokes
& the thing came loose,
I dragged it
across the drive.
Where it had fallen
dead undergrowth
came to light
first time in years.
It was good
to cut.
I brought the saw back
to the garage,
did not bother
to pick out of its
teeth the shreds of white wood.
Good to hack,
better to get
the wood cleared away.
*Against gardens:*
To break
the caressive
shades.
        Branchwork.
Ramas, boscas, pájaros
in the moon. Bird
in the bush.
        I see light
through the fingers,
flare
through meat. I nod
my head
to the necessary Force,
Goddess, Parca, Kali
of energy restor'd,
shakti silked in red.

I knew now

where I had to lead her,
to bring her home
into the most
open space.
Only what grows
by itself
has value.

If I sent her out
into an idea
she would come home
barren,
        if I went with her
past the lonely
phosphorescent
belt of the moon
(she wears dark
nights, against
the blundering planets,
safety on roads,
safe
      at every crossing)
she would come with me
& both of us
awaken
from the need of gardens.
Eden
was to be left.
With one throw
of our immaculate
bodies
we were past
its gates.
Goodbye Sun.
Matter
meant

to be known.
Eccentric
courses
of our truest
need:
      to be everything.
To come back
so armed
no garden
could enclose,
the old white-
limed walls
crumble
& the garden
is the world.

Only my eyes
had to see it,
had to go beyond
the place I left her
to see her again.
We leave
to find.
We go out
to come home.
And *Ile unarme again*
& lay me down
to the woman's
doom,
her changeable
self-images,
the dark
of what she hardly
knows herself to want.
And that will be my downfall
from which I'll rise,

giving no one any garden
but good day,
                    a word
on the other side of the wall.

The Hero
cuts his breastplate loose
& stands before her naked;
his eyes
locked in his head
find a letter
she has left:
*while you lingered*
*in the garden*
*I was up & away —*
*dont count on me*
*for your fall,*
*I am no man's ruin.*
*Find me*
*in your chemicals.*
He holds
his hands
flat to his breasts,
turns blue,
the color of moonlight
in green leaves.
He is mottled
with shadow
but his skin
is very bright.
He lets out his breath
& is a woman,
the red serpents
writhe up his spine
& bomb his head
with their darting

faces, their tongues
burn out his mind.
They coil around
his pineal gland,
uncurl, pour down
over the pituitaries
& enter his throat
tasting like tears.
They find him out
down there
where he is weakest now
from the night-time change.
His knees tremble
& he drops to his knees.
His eyes
see nothing
at last.
He falls back,
calf under thigh,
his body arched
till the back of his head
is on the grass,
the serpents
come back to his throat
& make him howl,
his hands clench
still on his breasts,
it is the door,
he beats on it,
an amber light
goes on, his heart
purples it, the snakes
for a little
are confused,
replace his lungs,
no breath,

                then dart
down again
& thrust out of him,
he becomes a man again
& no one
comes to the door.
He relaxes,
the grass is cool.
What he called upon
did not answer.
Would not answer
as long as he kept
the cock of his mind
locked
in his red garden.
He knew that,
but would he change.
There was nothing to him
but the changing.
The sun.
The oxen, delivered
to his teeth.
The road up. Metabolism.
The basket & boxes.
The honeycomb. The reed.
He felt his body
was made of music
& that made him easy
in the dark of
what he wasnt doing.
The duty was flesh
& just to be there.
Simple, so as to pass
the clumsy gestures
of his understanding.
He felt the music

& was content with it.
All the irrelevance
of which he was scholar
came to unmind him
of what was proposed.
Let her find herself first,
he thought, & then find me.
Above him some leaves
he thought were holly.
With that word
safe in his mind
he fell on sleep.

The two girls
found him
that way at dawn.
–At least
he's gotten out,
one said.
And the other:
Only halfway.
The first
took lipstick
& wrote God's name
across his forehead.
The other wondered
if he would chance
to see himself
before it rubbed away,
or read it right.
Still wondering
she followed her sister
out of his sleeping mind.

# 30

It fell.
Petals
when the clock
I couldnt see
said fall
fell,
two of them,
ten of them
before I go
to count,
lying
in the foreground
of a Brahms
quintet.
I knock
a couple more down,
one goes
to the floor,
on my way
to pick it up
& smell
what's left,
the water
in the glass
tinted

"Thus one tincture colors metals. These discover-
ies have given rise to the idea that one substance
can be transformed into another, so that a rough,

coarse and beshitten substance can be transmu-
ted into one that is pure, refined, and sound.
Such results I have attained in various kinds, al-
ways in connection with attempts to change me-
tals into gold and silver."

Gentle heat.
Give rise
to an idea.
Give a lie.
The redskin doubts
marauding from the hills.
Last night
you were so passive,
what did it mean,
the whole thing
gone too quiet
in my arms.
Too quiet?
A gentle heat
of those parts
we are most
generous.

The sniper on the rooftop
is the loneliest Eros,
not even a window
to enclose him,
a sky
with him in it
like a dove,
            quiet,
part of the weather.
"Oh that's all right,
my insecurity
is only sexual. . ."

Too quiet.
And doubting the ardor,
wake up to implant
the doubt-seed
in the time of my mind:
Release the stone,
the sexual deed
from generation.

My one-eye, mi tuerto,
unlidded,
Polyphemus
(Much-Talking)
between the thighs.
Consumed everything
came his way.
Till No-One
put his eye out,
i.e., balked
his generative frenzy
so he floundered
in the sea
at first for revenge
& later
for the wet of it,
the exact
delight.
Now Poseidon was his father.
Until he met the hero
he was hung on progeny —
called sheep
in the story,
mindless infants
of their father's
unfocused will.
But then the blinding:

subincision,
vulva opened
in the male's flesh,
so he knew all the world
as lust
& no cause
to confuse.
The sheep grew up
& he went to sea.
Where the story leaves him,
on his way.
As God be my wetness.
Across the sea of dolphins
into the rock womb
where the bees wove
combs for their honey,
ate their honey
(mel maris, sea's
honey) all down
& his head lit up
with a good idea.
Red, the color of
the tip of his tongue.
His enlightened mind
forgave his senses
for being more numerous
than he had long supposed.
Then the dolphins
courted his wits
& flattered his emergence
into the swill
left over from the sea
& his first scratchings
at the notion of land,
his isles
began to congregate,

touched,
          a continent began.
Of my incontinence
o Great Wet God (he cried)
I have established.
Yachin. I have made
the twist
          in the fiber
of the tree, bast, twist,
raffia, skirts
to hide my motherpart,
I twisted my foreskin
& a mountain appeared,
she spoke to me & now
Wet Father
I squelch my footsteps,
hear me, on this new land.
I plod up these contents
with a will to solid,
I gather my remarks
from the aimless
hootings of your sea.
I twist the fibers
to declare: this
is the genetic
of being free,
          the code
of outwards. Hear me
or no matter,
I language this place.

In his right palm
he found
the formula for fire,
spoke it, kindled
& a new light

offered over his idea —
it's just a big island.
He blew on it
& the people came
out of the ground
beating pots & blowing
their horns, came out
like ants but unlike ants
each different in size
& essential dignity.
He made his fire
out of water
& encouraged them to speak.
"You all have eyes
to see for yourselves."
Thus he spoke.
His words
wove vegetation
on earth,
opened the mouths
of leaves,
coaxed veins to rise
all through the high
trees.
        "It's about time
we created a world
for all you people
to move around in
& make sense of."
Beginnings
of a dialectic.
Trumpet call,
confused listeners
anxious to get back to their lives.
And Polyphemus moves
with new grace

stretching his giant form
over the vulvary hollows of
other people's lives.
Demiourgos. Maker
in a blind
          pain of making,
centering a world
out of his hunger to declare.

Sometimes the shape is lost.
Sometimes it has no shape.
Propositional,
the snowfall three thousand miles
from where I'm sitting
hunched over the
sight of a banana tree.
Only the fruit
from my own soil
can heal me,
exigent stone.
Demand
of this place.
Sometimes I catch a glimpse of it
everywhere.
What I have made
I made from lust
for eternal conditions,
open systems;
eternity.
          Which is at war
with time,
with the way things are.
But the way things are
is the only gate,
if you had no body
you'd be no where.

And here I stand
behind my eyes
weaving my own way
out & in.

Enclosed by nothing
he stands in the sky
taking aim
with blind eye –
how can he do anything
but make a world
the way things are
since he is guided
only by the gist of things
as they come to hand,
nothing wrong with his hands,
he is obedient
to the forms of things
but cannot see them.
He is excluded
from any world he makes
since his only reality
is making them.
Making.
          And I who am made
strong
with the fibers
he gives me to weave
can move in his garden
& see beyond it.
Looking for nothing.

The marksman
sees less than any man.
He has fallen
from his rooftop

into the work of his eyes,
his eye
on the sight,
he's nowhere
& his only answer
is the aim he takes,
the bullet
falls down,
hits or misses,
there is no magic
in his sudden deaths
or world after world
too quickly
summoned into being
out of the wild
beautiful chaos
it should be our
honor to inhabit.
Quick
        to every chance
& all the etceteras
rising & twining
faster than birds.
The sacred language
syllable by syllable
into your ear,
                known best
when you're hardly listening.

# 31

To find the natural houses of things
inside & out,
             to pick up the first
        tree-fall lemon, little,
almost all yellow, still
faint with green,
              to
have believed in these things
             beyond necessity
& make a virtue of
this granted earth,
           & then to heal all that
in the first oven,
            the mechanic forms burn,
their ash
yields human life
on the other side of society

& that life too is for burning.

# 32

The cat
for wash
her paw
a little
lifted,
a little bit
above
what we
mutually
stand up on,
a stance
to be herself
& move the quicker
up from the long
pull.
Levity. A cat
as man,
an harpsichord,
quills lifted
to induce
friction upon
percussion,
       the sound
knows itself.
Comes to consciousness.
'The wise will be ruled by stars?'
Or will himself
lead the stars
into his meadow,

'his' for his efforts,
shepherd's lien
on all this grass.
To feed the nice
animals he is,
& feed on them
with all the others
he is. And she is.
And the cat
can leap. Shall I
without mechanic form
leap up?
The machine
has friendship in it,
good shepherd, Angel,
who induces in me
a certain friction
from which the conscious
lets itself be born.
That's flower, trolley-car,
sun-filled streets of our
history,
            the twist
of knowingness.
Nothing discovered. No wind
from the Antipodes.
This round city
where we came
to work something out,
& still it goes, hung
on body or in body,
this four-footed dream
of what our original energies
were meant to know,
                        trapped
in the web of symbols meant

as map of how to get Out.
Goodbye Herod! I am tired
of your tyrant deserts,
I pick myself up
& travel
over a barely remembered
road southwest,
my brain
knocking its way
out of my skull,
into Egypt,
that princely escape,
in fact to come home
where all the parables began
by the river of Work
leading in its upper
reaches to the Winter Sunstead,
the doors of Capricorn
blown open by this
chrono-chemical compound,
this body
burning its now
on the doorsill
of the final gate.
Nile is naked
& we so innocent
likewise ascending,
raft or boat of reeds,
my hair the sail,
farewell, bees!
farewell, winter wheat!

# 33

I hailed him then
after long neglect
to call out precisely
the nature of his
location now
veered a moment closer
to my visible eyes
Saturn entering Gemini
& Pluto run now to renew
our sense of law in Libra,
the house we shared
not choosing to, choosing
later, after all,
to come home to one place,
north, in mist, Neptune
overhead. Well then —
I have watched the pictures
your words cast
on the bare walls of my mind,
the least I can do
is say hello, pass the time
of day with you, passing
the rim of the orbit
by which you sometimes return,
best of stars, your light
is much on our minds now.
And he: "Delight
was my only instruction.
Everything else

was gratuitous nonsense
from feigned masters.
Delight in the doing
or making or
handling of things was all
the sense I had: it sufficed,
it postulated a tradition
of intense Use, began one,
carried on. Nobody ever
carried on like me.
Here is Frederick, our emperor,
& here beside me a poet
to amend my craft, who teaches me
slowly you cant make
fire as you'd make a carpet,
it isnt formula, it isnt
a regular weave. Out here,
there is still to learn.
And still to burn."
Wherewith he continued
sideways on the mountain
between his companions
(not visible to me
except as inferences from
his words & hands, moving
kindly as he moved)
in search of the confident cave
his studies had foretold.
Once he turned round
& cried me: "Before Equal Night
I will be there!"
Carried before him
the branch has flowered,
young boys carry it
to a place like Rome,
anyway on a river,

some hills, an old man
welcomes the rumor
of his coming, hails him,
*Diener und Sohn*,
the branch has purple
scarlet flowers, they grow
from the sense of him as woman,
as winner, first footstep
out of the Easter tomb,
the flower
taste of stone, of wind, wind
flower, I watch him go.
We are healed
of our resemblance.
But the mountain
was sideways
to any movement.
Everything I had hoped
was simple,
to have the health
to go on. We sick men,
nous malandains —
old word, how the plague
came down
& knew our bodies,
or knew the Asia
in us, the fester-cities
trained to exult
in heat & disease
for the sake of the colors:
pink, pistachio, the gold
brown of turmeric
smeared on our doors.
Our? That mistake comes back.
I am alone on the mountain.
The comradeship

is a matter of few words,
a sign, a look
as we severally go,
the mountain
also moves.
Its minerals
are condescension, its grass
is memory.
               What does this mean.
I forget.  I found it
beside me when I woke,
embedded in a kind of pain,
a mother-lode of awkwardness
wanting to get out. Out
is where the mountain goes.
Conspiracies.
General Delivery.
Lost the last trace of her,
made sense to,
I can live
only in the present.
On the mountain.
Then I grew old
& doubted the science of Numbers.
I doubted the woman
in her own cave, I doubted
the girl on the corner —
no night
has such a dark hotel. Corner!
Myriad wheats!
If I could do that would you love me?
If I could remember would you
reconstitute yourself in my
bones? get inside me?
once & for all?
               These idle questioners

scratched
& tolerated the mountain
for its declivities. Now they moved off
west, like all the rest,
still scratching, making sure
their hemlines attuned
with sunset horizon. Grand Canyon.
A hole through the world, marching.
Vesica Piscis. Or what I see
when I hold my palms together
& sight between them:
womanshape, girlscape, the world
is worth it! it matters!
it begins!
        & the questioners
look like prickly pears
in silhouette, down there,
shadows, why do they go down?
The girls move & the cactuses
hardly, the mountain & I go on.
Kabbalah
is reception.

Then all my ladies came,
moving together
like a wall carved
full of breasts & hips & hands
reaching
out of the bright colors
that hide the stone.
One spoke: "Come
among my companions
who have waited
for your movie to begin
a thousand years.
If we're going to get

some action, we're bound
to need some madness, come
sleek your languid derangements
over our calm hair,
pour in, pour in,
it's only crazy,
your Oil of Frenzy
& Silly Salts,
pour in, we're only
angels, only the girls
you tunneled through in Carbondale,
bridge girls, only the shadows
you mistook for us
(paradox!) in filthy rivers
that sparkle through
the indecent cities you imagine.
Linden leaves! Sycamore!
I am the immediate voice,
imperative, present
in all your active,
middle, turning the worm
of you passive, I insist,
I am inchoative
when you lie down with anyone,
hear me, I am the inevitable
& my sisters likewise
can be no part
of your derangement, just
audience, we sit in the temple
darkened with your images
tricky against the pure light.
You command us
from the candy stand
& the scandalous drinking fountain,
we arise on griffin-back
our white limbs

smirched in balconies,
we are old-fashioned,
it's all an opera, we sing
your way into confusion,
there is no path
for your swans to waddle
free of our influence. Yes!
It is a castle!
You saw me come down the stairs
discarding my clothes,
you cried out o Holy
Wood where such Maidens
give themselves over to my eyes
trusting in my capacity
to heal them with my Vision!
You did. We heard you.
You cant squirm out of it now —
you are committed
to see us as divine
since in a passion of intellectual
diversion you cast all others out.
We are your gods.
Kneel on the sticky red carpet
& hear our immense Measurements
expanded for your sake
into Kabbalah, Most Meaningful Work,
How To Do It, Your Instructions,
Book of the Inside of Your Head.
Get down & pray!"

-You are not gods, I cried out,
you are heaven,
you are where gods are,
uranian ones, you are the Place
which art in heaven
but are no one,

as I have been taught
by all the men who went
before me on this mountain.

But none of them were there
to help me bear that witness.
Just these apsarases
& daughters of music
with other high-flown figures
across the sky of my
naiver expectations. I love them.
I love you. I love you.
House of my need.
Sidereal code, solved in your
opening thighs.

One sterner than the rest
came to the front of the troupe
& frowning reported: "We have heard
all that before.
Yours is a mental frenzy
compounded of numbers & calendars
& like all quantifying emotions
is glued to its apparent object —
you lose
the energy we are.
The energy
that is our racial difference
perceived,
our beauty is unlikeness,
unlikeliness."

With all the calm
I gathered from her rock
I waved my arms & said
softly, softly

"Depart.
For all I love you, go,
the particular
is always angular."
And I am gone.

# 34

And moved
always
to the corner
always waited
for the bus.
The place I stand
lies on the furthest avenue
down which it has to come.
And will there be room?
Around my life
an animal paces
alternate
in the shadows of leaves,
a beast whose skin
seems all of mouths.

West up the street
the squat civilian bus
passes some cars,
threads close.
The sun sets
inside it,
the whole vehicle
filled with light.
The creature's circle
closes in,
the corner where I wait
gets smaller,
the gutter

deepens with water,
all the fish of my life
swim by.
A woman
lifts from the shallows
an egg to me
bright in her small wet hand—
"You dropped this
long ago,
you thought it was a dream
or worthless creed
but look,
I rise to you
to restore."
—An egg
to pay my fare?
This is not my coin.
I go too far
for this liberty.
Time is my enemy.

I had spoken to an empty road
across which now I see
it is a fox
waiting
part way up the mountain.
"All the other animals
had me in mind,
believe none of them,
go free,
drop the egg
& come with me."

I cupped my hand to my mouth
to hear her better.
She moved up

always looking back.
I crossed no road
& climbed no fence,
I followed,
I have always followed.
The whole city
twanged
in the heart of my head,
faded
in the fact
of the mountain.
The eyes she looked
back at me
knew all the words
I was like to say.

"Time?" she said,
"the wasted hours
become your only song."

# 35

Now then at last
the voice
I kept talking
to provoke
spoke:
-What *do* you want?
-I want to learn the prayer
I must say in this place.
-Must? -Because the Aire
to which I've wandered
has a need for prayer, an old
lingo, a megaHertz connection
between my various heads, savvy?
-I have always & every
where savvied everything
that could be of use to you.
Now pray with me: *Patêr hêmôn*
that is Source
from which we come,
called Father, active
in her will now
active in ours, not our
father but father of us
—this focuses
what you mean to say, say it
to the top of yourself
or mother
from which you're coming
& with luck to go,

*ho*, who is particular,
referential & relates
to you as a specific
only, no general, no mist
in that specific
focus of light,
diamondwise in the furrow between —
*en tois ouranois*
in those excelsitudes,
plural, altitudes
called heavens, one
for each man perhaps &
all for one, high
places above my heads
or in them, & in them —
wild bedrooms
above the conscious house,
the attic workshop
where my life is made —
Master of this House
*hagiasthêtô to onoma sou*
if I keep reverence
always
for your names & works
my sense of the Day
will open,
will fill with you
& draw you to me
with all your power
to change & exchange
& come,
            *elthatô*
*hê basileia sou*
set the rule of your just
proportion, life
of meaning, over the jests

I trick out with my
hungers, let me be conscious
all ways, as you are
conscious.
As there is no one but you
to be conscious.
*Genêthêtô to thelêma sou*
your will happen
to our place, my
place is in, let the will
that is my turn
to live be yours, let your will
be done
so we can have no will
*hôs en ouranô*
as it is always being being
in the high places, so let it
*kai epi gês –*
            also on earth,
that the old relation
be maintained,
                as above so below,
to let me find your will
in everyday places, not a game,
no midnight fabulation
but the work of morning,
bring it down
into my life
            or let it
know me.
This is a conformity:
that the mechanic forms
of sleepy daytime
match (when? at noon?)
the bionic forms of
all my life, all

our lives, the whole
shape of heaven
to know its times
& get free of them.
Because we live in time
give us today
something beyond it
that we can keep in mind,
that we can eat
the taste of outside time
that it
become me,
                    *Ton arton*
*hêmôn ton epiousion*
*dos hêmin sêmeron,*
give us the bread beyond substance
& give it to us
because in some way it's ours,
because there is an us
beyond substance too.
Or there's nothing beyond us
except not to be
the machine I am —
metabolize me that way
*kai aphes hêmin ta opheilêmata hêmôn*
& forget the things we owe
*hôs kai hêmeis aphêkamen tois opheiletais hêmôn*
in exact measure with how we
forgive our debtors, those
I suppose to owe me something.
This is the only thing
the prayer makes me
undertake to do. Do it. For
give each debtor,
make the debt
nothing in my mind —

*kai mê eisenegkês hêmas*
*eis peirasmon,* & do not lead us
into trial *alla rhusai hêmas*
*apo tou ponêrou* but snatch us
from the Burdener, that coward
filled with accusation
who walks the streets of my life
blaming me & thee & everyone
with my tongue, who sets men
in the phony wars, makes them
hate each other & begin
the longest sleep again.
He stirs us to dream.
Every doubt
is part of his mystery.

# 36

The leaf
I lent you,
            where is that now,
you who were so bold
as to put cities behind you?

Only a loan at best,
the light reclaims our eyes.
Re-possession. The credit
of our movement. A death
for Robert, to elicit life.

Skull on desk, my hand's
independent fingers rest
on suture. Ape
over my head, blank stare
of a creature-world
that does not imagine death.

Dried stalk of cholla
Ted left us, caduceus
of desert places. Snake
with seven mouths. To hold
the water of our lights in,
to redeem our eyes.
Lace ruff collar
to hold my heavy head up,
where have I seen the like?

South is my destruction.
Do not move south.
Powerline. Firebreak. Up
the implicit canyon, *sulca*,
where a girl named Helen is
for a flicker the shape of my.
Input.
               The work
starts in the conviction of death.
Not somebody else's —
no murderers need apply.
The shape of my death
like a furrow like a Helen like a
firebreak a warp in the mountains
crock of andesite beginning to shift.
Earthquake. Venereal
contagion. *L'aura* plagued,
with influences many,
settling down to a long story
she reads in me.
And the dawn.
Which for all its light
is not certainly clear.

Sweat it out. Which
direction has the music in?
North was always
where I wanted.
Set out the oracle
eye turned to the blind inside
hoping. The hopping
frog-like people come
waving their reminders —
a pain in the ass
but their fingers are lucky,
count them, they flicker

& communicate
what they learned
under the mountain.
The animal sleeps.

A broad plain
not easy to see, drifts
of mist on it,
but the movements
arent all in the air,
something on the ground
has its own directions,
connections, does
not approach me.
Wrap the stole around me,
pick up the cup.
Whatever that is down there
I know it for my loss
or I its master
prone to fall down.
I laugh, because a rock.

The bird was black
but now not even shadows
throw that color. The bird
is yellow, flicks
from rock to rock,
I follow, with the writing
in my hands, reading,
hurrying, I do not stumble
even once. The bird
is on a dead oak tree
or is it winter. I wonder.
I followed
wherever it flew,
it would be tedious

to examine the joys
I experienced therein,
the sure direction, constant
pursuit, its speed
tempered to my
reading rate, sometimes
I ran.
Up the arms of the cross
& down the star's
fleshy arms
right into the hands
of a candle —
I should have stayed
among the rams,
nothing to do
but love real women.
But now I hastened
over this unlikely plain
lit by the glow
that forced itself
out of my heart,
a consort of pains
lighting up
wheels of my body,
*rotae*, the turns
that gave off light
inside me —
that was the strangeness
in running,
that I was source
of the only light
& source of the running too.
I could do as well
to stand still. I did
& the lights went out.
Wherever the valley

was coming from it
wasnt from me.
There was only that stone
place & laughable rock,
how could I care
about that
& yet I did,
my pockets filled
since morning
with dried chips of meat
written on
with fat soft lead pencil
the sigils of powers
I imagined to preside
over the planetary
hours of the day I
thought it was.
I ate one every two
human hours & needed water —
isnt that history?
I kept talking I mean
walking now, trying
to keep cool, a wind
up to meet me & indeed
I wasnt on the level yet.
But my efforts brought
the light back, dimmer now
from the ingested food.
I tried to vomit
& got a black ball of slime
in a ribbon of acid yellow —
is this my food?
I thought I had left such
in the valley of crows.
On the other side.
But I felt better

going on, lighter
for emptiness.
Kept going down along.
But interruptions
ran my charge
down. Feeble battery
I run on,
head in heaven
whisk
of pure reason
& purer feeling
sweep the sky
blue again.
                    Dark
earth & bright heaven.
BUILD MY TEMPLE
in the shape of
this body,
size of this kind.


It was the lowlands
at last,
            sea-level —
tongue in mouth
at rest.
Every work of a man
starts at sea-level —
only later
to the mountains.

Sea's face,
the membrane we are.

Now there was
clear space to work in.
I was there, & knew it

because I'd stopped moving.
It was the place
because it was place.
I could stand up or lie down.
The stars. The sequences
of life on earth,
what I knew nothing about,
what I dimly guessed,
what was on
the tip of my tongues,
the sentences. The books.
All I ever knew
was how to know
what some other
was thinking of.
Or all I knew
was to do. This.

Three times
I walked around it,
the place I knew it was,
until my feet
got the feel of the
shape of it.
Contact with ground.
And most of the time
for all my dreams
I moved cautiously,
trying to be humble
to the place, not to think
about it too much,
to know it
as it might let
itself be known
or as I would let,
sometimes, a woman

know me.  In *time,*
that great Bed
of dailiness,
utter intimacy
of going on.
But slowly,
letting the ground
know me too,
as it would, or shape
my walking on it.
Maybe I spent too long
but the only time
was what I happened
to be doing; at length
it was done.
I marked the boundary,
an enclosure
of three sides, its fourth
a semicircle curved out
towards the horizon
away from the hills.
Perhaps east.  The sun
came roughly that way.
A smaller enclosure
on the west,
adjoining the blunt end.

Then from the upper
left, way
back in my head,
the quarry, I lifted
blocks of grey stone,
set them out
end to end
along the boundary —
just one course

along the ground,
but enough
to set the place off,
mark it.  Enclose.
The blocks were heavy,
had to drag them
out & across, always
fetching from the left,
behind me almost,
dragging & pushing
to get them in line.
Most days I could manage
ten, then lay down
to sleep in the smaller
chamber I foresaw.
The last part I worked on
was the semicircle,
& when that was finished
it was the first wall proper
I coaxed to rise,
the stones smaller now
so I could lift them,
grunting, into place.
When this curved wall
or apsidial was
as high as my heart
I left off work on it
& went back to the rest.
After some weeks I'd raised
a wall of one height
all round the enclosures,
leaving a gap only
in the west wall
& another facing it
between the smaller
& the larger rooms.

Something told me,
maybe the way
the birds were drifting back,
that the rains were coming
so I worked faster.
Towards the eastern end
in the bay or curve
I set two pillars up
making them as high
as I could lift the stones.
Between them
but set a little back,
the altar
high as my genitals
& with a square top
half as wide
as the altar was high.

These things I measured
in the doubt of time
using the yardsticks
my body gave me
& the shadows
each stone or construct
cast — from those
I learned direction.
I had no wish
to impose.
I found it
as it was
& sometimes prayed it
to make me its
or find a way
to mark me
as my stonework
had declared it.

When I had done
what I wanted
& what I could,
dark clouds appeared
so I hastened to gather
certain plants,
wormwoods, fleshy
parts of cactus,
southernwood
from a dry place
back up the hill,
white sage, black sage,
leaves of manzanita.
All these I steeped
overnight in brackish
water in a hollowed rock.
When I woke
the rain was there.
I drank down the potion
& sucked the pulp
to get all I could
of what they mattered.
Then it was my business
to lie in the rain,
face up, at the base
of the altar. I knew
that the fresh rain,
three days of it
I counted on, would wash
something out of my flesh
I had no need
to keep inside,
& my face be washed
& its structure change.
Lay there except for when
that potion

churning inside me
made me run outside,
cleaned me out,
bloody flux
then peace again
to lie in the rain.
After the three days
appointed, the sun
came back.  I waited
while it dried
what it could,
then arose from the mud
& walked out,
around the walls
three times.
Let the sun in
always, let her in.
My face felt strange,
I had to lie
all those days in rain
not moving my face,
sometimes opening my lips
to drink.  The sun
dried.  I felt fever
in me, the plan
I read in the ground
was working.
While the mud inside
was still wet,
I plastered it
all over the left-hand
pillar, then went down
to the alkali spring
to wash myself clean
one last time.
The salts

dried on my hands & arms,
I scratched at them,
the fever mounted.
Back at the altar
I kissed its top
& breathed on it
in the shape of cross
I guessed was right.
Closed my eyes,
moved three steps west
& sat on the ground
facing the altar.
When I opened my eyes
I found to my
satisfaction
that my skull
had slipped out of my head
& sat on the altartop
looking at me.
This is the first
of my offerings.
The skull
had eyes of its own
& watched me
with their color
not my own, the opposite
of my own.
I wondered who or what
was in my head;
I felt my forehead,
supple curves
of cheeks & temples.
I was cooler now,
quiet, watched
my Death up there
watch me.

It began to talk
& comment on the colors,
the black, the white,
the yellow, & how
they were not enough,
good enough in their time
but gone now. I was
impatient, I knew that.
Its voice
was also like birds,
as if a dozen
had gotten together
to fashion the parts of words,
vowels, stops, sibilants,
stresses rapped out.
It spoke to me
& when it did
blood began to spread
over its white dome.
*It is time & past time*
*& the beginning of time —*
*you have no one but me*
*to show you the way*
*but I can bring you close,*
*or close enough. I am more*
*than enough.* It spoke to me
that way, & when I looked away,
distracted by a bird,
woodpecker or whatever,
over on the wall,
I looked back to find
the skull no longer there.
I understood
it had come back
inside my head
& would for the most part

continue there, would
lead me.  I could feel
Death trying to shape
my dry lips, dry throat,
as if to speak.
But maybe then
it wasnt important to speak.
I was very thirsty
& went to the spring,
aiming to gather water
& let it settle
in the hollow rock
till all the salts
precipitated out.
Then I could drink.
Outside I found all round me
that the desert had
predictably but to my surprise
after the heavy rain &
warmed now by the sun
crashed into flower.
I even had to walk on some
to get to the well,
small ones, very bright red.

Printed August 1975 in Santa Barbara & Ann Arbor for the
Black Sparrow Press by Noel Young & Edwards Brothers
Inc. Typography by Helen in Annandale. Design by Barbara
Martin. This edition is published in paper wrappers; there
are 250 numbered & signed hardcover copies. Fifty copies
have been hand-bound in boards by Earle Gray, & each
contains an original illumination by the author.

Photo: *Layle Silbert*

Robert Kelly was born in 1935 in Brooklyn. Since 1961 he has published thirty or more books and pamphlets, most of them poetry, a few prose. Black Sparrow has published ten of his books, most recently *The Common Shore* (1969), *Flesh Dream Book* (1971), and *The Mill of Particulars* (1973). *The Loom* was composed in 1971 and 1972 while the author was Poet in Residence at the California Institute of Technology, and extensively revised during 1973-1975. Robert Kelly teaches at Bard College, and lives with his wife Helen in Annandale.